WANDERLUST

WANDERLUST

A
Travel Anthology

Compiled by
ROY LACEY

With drawings by
J. YUNGE-BATEMAN

WINCHESTER PUBLICATIONS LIMITED
16 MADDOX STREET LONDON W.1

Published in mcmxlviii by
Winchester Publications Limited
16 Maddox Street, London W.1

Made and printed in Great Britain
by Purnell and Sons Limited
Paulton (Somerset) and London

CONTENTS

The extracts of prose and poetry in this anthology are arranged in eight parts which are intended to be read consecutively. Each part is concerned with one aspect of the traveller's progress, but each is linked by a continuous theme. It is the compiler's hope that this pattern will assist the reader in making an ordered but adventurous passage through the book.

R. L.

DEPARTURE

Setting Off

THE NEXT morning was Saturday, and a breeze having sprung up from the southward, we took a pilot on board, hove up our anchor, and began beating down the bay. I took leave of those of my friends who came to see me off, and had barely opportunity to take a last look at the city, and well-known objects, as no time is allowed on board ship for sentiment. As we drew down into the lower harbour, we found the wind ahead in the bay, and were obliged to come to anchor in the roads. We remained there through the day and a part of the night.

My watch began at eleven o'clock at night, and I received orders to call the captain if the wind came out from the westward. About midnight the wind became fair, and having called the captain, I was ordered to call all hands. How I accomplished this I do not know, but I am quite sure that I did not give the true hoarse, boatswain call of " A-a-ll ha-a-a-nds! up anchor, a ho-oy! " In a short time every one was in motion, the sails loosed, the yards braced, and we began to heave up the anchor, which was our last hold upon Yankee land.

I could take but little part in all these preparations. My little knowledge of a vessel was all at fault. Unintelligible orders were so rapidly given, and so immediately executed; there was such a hurrying about, and such an intermingling of strange cries and stranger actions, that I was completely bewildered. There is not so helpless and pitiable an object in the world as a landsman beginning a sailor's life. At length those peculiar, long-drawn sounds, which denote that the crew are heaving the windlass, began, and in a few moments we were under weigh. The noise of the water thrown from the bows began to be heard, the vessel leaned over from the damp night-breeze, and rolled with the heavy ground swell, and we had actually begun our long, long journey. This was literally bidding " good night " to my native land.

R. H. Dana, Jun.

3

Why Do You Stay?

WHY DO you stay here and live this mean moiling life when a glorious existence is possible for you? These same stars twinkle over other fields than these.

H. D. Thoreau

ALTHOUGH OUR ordinary air be good by nature or art, yet it is not amiss, as I have said, still to alter it; no better Physick for a melancholy man, than change of air, and variety of places, to travel abroad and see fashions.

Robert Burton

IT IS injurious to the mind as well as to the body to be always in one place and always surrounded by the same circumstances. A species of thick clothing slowly grows about the mind, the pores are choked, little habits become a part of existence, and by degrees the mind is inclosed in a husk.

Richard Jefferies

THERE IS nobody under thirty so dead but his heart will stir a little at sight of a gypsies' camp. " We are not cotton-spinners all "; or, at least, not all through. There is some life in humanity yet; and youth will now and again find a brave word to say in dispraise of riches, and throw up a situation to go strolling with a knapsack.

R. L. Stevenson

I Have Desired To Go

I HAVE desired to go
   Where springs not fail,
To fields where flies no sharp and sided hail,
   And a few lilies blow.

And I have asked to be
   Where no storms come,
Where the green swell is in the havens dumb,
   And out of the swing of the sea.

Gerard Manley Hopkins

The Caravan Rolls On

HAVE WE not envied—futile though it be—
Those navigators of an early day,
When half the world in shadow-garments lay
And high romance was heard on every quay?
But now there is no island in the sea
That is unknown, unvisited, we say.
Now shrunken is the world, how dull and grey
The time that is devoid of mystery.
Yet there are countries calling us to scan
Their populations and we penetrate
Into the twilight of the soul of man,
To find a desert or some fair estate—
So let the bells ring of our caravan,
Whatever on the road may lie in wait.

Henry Baerlein

Of Travel

TRAVEL, in the younger sort, is a part of education; in the elder, a part of experience. He that travelleth into a country before he hath some entrance into the language, goeth to school, and not to travel. That young men travel under some tutor, or grave servant, I allow well; so that he be such a one that hath the language and hath been in the country before; whereby he may be able to tell them what things are worthy to be seen in the country where they go; what acquaintances they are to seek; what exercises or discipline the place yieldeth. For else young men shall go hooded, and look abroad little. It is a strange thing that in sea-voyages, where there is nothing to be seen but sky and sea, men should make diaries, but in land-travel, wherein so much is to be observed, for the most part they omit it; as if chance were fitter to be registered than observation. Let diaries, therefore, be brought in use.

The things to be seen and observed are: the courts of princes, specially when they give audience to ambassadors; the courts of justice, while they sit and hear causes, and so of consistories ecclesiastic; the churches and monasteries, with the monuments which are therein extant; the walls and fortifications of cities and towns, and so the havens and harbours; antiquities and ruins; libraries; colleges, disputations, and lectures, where any are; shipping and navies; houses and gardens of state and pleasure, near great cities; armories; arsenals; magazines; exchanges; burses; warehouses; exercises of horsemanship, fencing, training of soldiers, and the like; comedies, such whereunto the better sort of persons do resort; treasuries of jewels and robes; cabinets and rarities; and, to conclude, whatsoever is memorable in the places where they go. After all which the tutors or servants ought to make diligent enquiry. As for triumphs, masques, feasts, weddings, funerals, capital executions, and such shews, men need not to be put in mind of them; yet they are not to be neglected.

If you will have a young man to put his travel into a little room, and in short time to gather much, this you must do. First, as was said, he must have some entrance into the language, before he goeth. Then he must have such a servant, or tutor, as knoweth the country, as was likewise said. Let him carry with him also some card or book describing the country where he travelleth; which will be a good key to his enquiry. Let him keep also a diary. Let him not stay long in one city or town; more or less as the place deserveth, but not long: nay, when he stayeth in one city or town, let him change his lodging from one end and part of the town to another; which is a great adamant of acquaintance. Let him sequester himself from the company of his countrymen, and diet in such places where there is good company of the nation where he travelleth. Let him, upon his removes from one place to another, procure recommendation to some person of quality residing in the place whither he removeth; that he may use his favour in those things he desireth to see or know. Thus he may abridge his travel with much profit. As for the acquaintance which is to be sought in travel; that which is most of all profitable is acquaintance with the secretaries and employed men of ambassadors; for so in travelling in one country he shall suck the experience of many. Let him also see and visit eminent persons in all kinds, which are of great name abroad; that he may be able to tell how the life agreeth with the fame. For quarrels, they are with care and discretion to be avoided: they are commonly for mistresses, healths, place, and words. And let a man beware how he keepeth company with choleric and quarrelsome persons; for they will engage him into their own quarrels.

When a traveller returneth home, let him not leave the countries where he hath travelled altogether behind him, but maintain a correspondence by letters with those of his acquaintance which are most worth. And let his travel appear rather in his discourse than in his apparel or gesture; and in his discourse let him be rather advised in his answers than forwards to tell stories; and let it appear that he doth not change his country manners for those of foreign parts, but only prick in some flowers of that he hath learned abroad into the customs of his own country.

Francis Bacon

Comus

To THE Ocean now I fly,
And those happy climes that lie
Where day never shuts his eye,
Up in the broad fields of the sky:
There I suck the liquid air
All amidst the Gardens fair
Of Hesperus, and his daughters three
That sing about the golden tree:
Along the crispèd shades and bowers
Revels the spruce and jocund Spring,
The Graces, and the rosy-bosom'd Hours,
Thither all their bounties bring;
There eternal Summer dwells,
And West winds, with musky wing,
About the cedar'n alleys fling
Nard and Cassia's balmy smells.
Iris there with humid bow,
Waters the odorous banks that blow
Flowers of more mingled hue
Than her purfl'd scarf can shew,
And drenches with Elysian dew
(List, mortals, if your ears be true)
Beds of Hyacinth, and roses
Where young Adonis oft reposes,
Waxing well of his deep wound
In slumber soft, and on the ground
Sadly sits th' Assyrian Queen;
But far above in spangled sheen
Celestial Cupid her fam'd son advanc'd
Holds his dear Psyche sweet entranc'd

After her wand'ring labours long,
Till free consent the gods among
Make her his eternal Bride,
And from her fair unspotted side
Two blissful twins are to be born,
Youth and Joy; so Jove hath sworn.
  But now my task is smoothly done,
I can fly, or I can run
Quickly to the green earth's end,
Where the bow'd welkin slow doth bend,
And from thence can soar as soon
To the corners of the Moon.
  Mortals that would follow me,
Love Virtue, she alone is free.
She can teach ye how to climb
Higher than the sphery chime;
Or if Virtue feeble were,
Heav'n itself would stoop to her.

John Milton

To Sea

To SEA! To sea! The calm is o'er;
The wanton water leaps in sport,
And rattles down the pebbly shore;
The dolphin wheels, the sea-cows snort,
And unseen Mermaids' pearly song
Comes bubbling up, the weeds among.
  Fling broad the sail, dip deep the oar:
To sea! To sea! The calm is o'er.

To sea! To sea! Our wide-winged bark
Shall billowy cleave its sunny way,
And with its shadow, fleet and dark,
Break the caved Tritons' azure ray,
Like mighty eagle soaring light
O'er antelopes on Alpine height.
  The anchor heaves, the ship swings free,
The sails swell full: To sea, to sea!

Thomas Lovell Beddoes

8

DEPARTURE

In Cabin'd Ships

Here are our thoughts, voyagers' thoughts,
Here not the land, firm land, alone appears, may then by them be said,
The sky o'erarches here, we feel the undulating deck beneath our feet,
We feel the long pulsation, ebb and flow of endless motion,
The tones of unseen mystery, the vague and vast suggestions of the briny
    world, the liquid-flowing syllables,
The perfume, the faint creaking of the cordage, the melancholy rhythm,
The boundless vista and the horizon far and dim are all here,
And this is ocean's poem.

Walt Whitman

On Shipboard

To TELL the truth there is something in the long, slow lift of the ship, and her long, slow slide forwards which makes my heart beat with joy. It is the motion of freedom. To feel her come up—then slide slowly forward, with the sound of the smashing of waters, is like the magic gallop of the sky, the magic gallop of elemental space. That long, slow, waveringly rhythmic rise and fall of the ship, with waters snorting as it were from her nostrils, oh, God, what a joy it is to the wild innermost soul. One is free at last—and lilting in a slow flight of the elements, winging outwards. Oh, God, to be free of all the hemmed-in life—the horror of human tension, the absolute insanity of machine persistence. The agony which a train is to me, really. And the long-drawn-out agony of a life among tense, resistant people on land. And then to feel the long, slow lift and drop of this almost empty ship, as she took the waters. Ah, God, liberty, liberty, elemental liberty. I wished in my soul the voyage might last for ever, that the sea had no end, that one might float in this wavering, tremulous, yet long and surging pulsation while ever time lasted: space never exhausted, and no turning back, no looking back, even.

D. H. Lawrence

Come, My Friends

THE LIGHTS begin to twinkle from the rocks:
The long day wanes: the slow moon climbs: the deep
Moans round with many voices. Come, my friends,
'Tis not too late to seek a newer world.
Push off, and, sitting well in order, smite
The sounding furrows; for my purpose holds
To sail beyond the sunset, and the baths
Of all the western stars, until I die.
It may be that the gulfs will wash us down:
It may be we shall touch the Happy Isles,
And see the great Achilles, whom we knew.
Tho' much is taken, much abides; and tho'
We are not now that strength which in old days
Moved heaven and earth; that which we are, we are;
One equal temper of heroic hearts
Made weak by time and fate, but strong in will
To strive, to seek, to find, and not to yield.

Lord Tennyson

Wander-Thirst

BEYOND THE East the sunrise, beyond the West the sea,
And East and West the wander-thirst that will not let me be;
It works in me like madness, dear, to bid me say good-bye;
For the seas call and the stars call, and oh! the call of the sky.

I know not where the white road runs, nor what the blue hills are,
But a man can have the Sun for friend, and for his guide a star;
And there's no end of voyaging when once the voice is heard,
For the river calls and the road calls, and oh! the call of a bird!

Yonder the long horizon lies, and there by night and day
The old ships draw to home again, the young ships sail away;
And come I may, but go I must, and, if men ask you why,
You may put the blame on the stars and the Sun and the white road
   and the sky.

Gerald Gould

The Young Crusoe

ON THE 1st of September, 1651, I went on board a ship bound for London. Never any young adventurer's misfortunes, I believe, began younger, or continued longer than mine. The ship had no sooner got out of the Humber, than the wind began to blow, and the waves to rise, in a most frightful manner; and as I had never been at sea before, I was most inexpressibly sick in body, and terrified in mind: I began now seriously to reflect upon what I had done, and how justly I was overtaken by the judgement of Heaven, for wickedly leaving my father's house. All the good counsels of my parents, my father's tears, and my mother's entreaties, came now fresh into my mind; and my conscience, which was not yet come to the pitch of hardness to which it has been since, reproached me with the contempt of advice, and the abandonment of my duty.

All this while the storm increased, and the sea, which I had never been upon before, went very high, though nothing like what I have seen many times since; no, nor what I saw a few days after; but, such as it was, enough to affect me then, who was but a young sailor, and had never known anything of the matter. I expected every wave would have swallowed us up, and that every time the ship fell down, as I thought, into the trough or hollow of the sea, we should never rise more; and in this agony of mind I made many vows and resolutions, that if it would please God to spare my life this voyage, if ever I got my foot once on dry land, I would go directly home to my father, and never set it into a ship again, while I lived; that I would take his advice, and never run myself into such miseries as these any more. Now I saw plainly the goodness of his observations about the middle station of life; how easy, how comfortable, he had lived all his days, and never had been exposed to tempests at sea or troubles on shore; and I resolved that I would, like a true repenting prodigal, go home to my father.

These wise and sober thoughts continued during the storm, and indeed some time after; but the next day, as the wind was abated, and the sea calmer, I began to be a little inured to it . . . and I entirely forgot the vows and promises I had made in my distress.

Daniel Defoe

Sea Lore

LICINIUS, trust a seaman's lore:
  Steer not too boldly to the deep,
Nor, fearing storms, by treacherous shore
    Too closely creep.
Who makes the golden mean his guide,
  Shuns miser's cabin, foul and dark,
Shuns gilded roofs, where pomp and pride
    Are envy's mark.
With fiercer blasts the pine's dim height
  Is rock'd; proud towers with heavier fall
Crash to the ground; and thunders smite
    The mountains tall.
In sadness hope, in gladness fear
  'Gainst coming change will fortify
Your breast. The storms that Jupiter
    Sweeps o'er the sky
He chases. Why should rain today
  Bring rain tomorrow? Python's foe
Is pleased sometimes his lyre to play,
    Nor bends his bow.
Be brave in trouble; meet distress
  With dauntless front; but when the gale
Too prosperous blows, be wise no less,
    And shorten sail.

Horace (trans. Dr. J. Conington)

Sunset at Sea

IT LOOKED as if it would be a long passage. The south-east trades, light and unsteady, were left behind; and then, on the equator and under a low grey sky, the ship, in close heat, floated upon a smooth sea that resembled a sheet of ground glass. Thunder squalls hung on the horizon, circled round the ship, far off and growling angrily, like a troop of wild beasts afraid to charge home. The invisible sun, sweeping above the upright masts, made on the clouds a blurred stain of rayless light, and a similar patch of faded radiance kept pace

with it from east to west over the unglittering level of the waters.
At night, through the impenetrable darkness of earth and heaven,
broad sheets of flames moved noiselessly; and for half a second the
becalmed craft stood out with its masts and rigging, with every sail
and every rope distinct and black in the centre of a fiery outburst, like
a charred ship enclosed in a globe of fire. And, again, for long hours
she remained lost in a vast universe of night and silence where gentle
sighs wandering here and there like forlorn souls, made the still sails
flutter as in sudden fear, and the ripple of a beshrouded ocean whisper
its compassion afar—in a voice mournful, immense, and faint . . .

Joseph Conrad

Boats at Night

How LOVELY is the sound of oars at night
   And unknown voices, borne through windless air,
From shadowy vessels floating out of sight
   Beyond the harbour lantern's broken glare
To those piled rocks that make on the dark wave
   Only a darker stain. The splashing oars
Slide softly on as in an echoing cave
   And with the whisper of the unseen shores
Mingle their music, till the bell of night
   Murmurs reverberations low and deep
That droop towards the land in swooning flight
   Like whispers from the lazy lips of sleep.
The oars grow faint. Below the cloud-dim hill
The shadows fade and now the bay is still.

Edward Shanks

Outward Bound

Where LIES the land to which yon ship must go ?
   Fresh as a lark mounting at break of day
   Festively she puts forth in trim array;
Is she for tropic suns, or polar snow ?
What boots the inquiry ?—Neither friend nor foe
She cares for; let her travel where she may,
   She finds familiar names, a beaten way
Ever before her, and a wind to blow.

Yet still I ask, what haven is her mark ?
And, almost as it was when ships were rare,
(From time to time, like pilgrims, here and there
Crossing the waters) doubt, and something dark,
Of the old sea some reverential fear,
Is with me at thy farewell, joyous bark!

William Wordsworth

Clipper Race

IT WAS mid-morning when we sighted Pitcairn Island. There was a piping wind and we were running fast. A little way astern another clipper followed. She'd been there yesterday, and all the starry night. She was so close that we could see the long lift and the pitch of her sharp cutwater, and almost hear the breaking music of her bow-wash. Pure white, her hull was. All her masts and spars and blocks and deck-houses were white. There was not anywhere a patch of colour on her. She was a tall white bird, fast hovering at our heel. Our Old Man scowled at her. And we scowled, too, fearing what he would do. Just thirty days we'd been at sea. The hard-tack was all weevils. The pork was rancid. Oh, pineapples, oh, oranges! And then of course, the Old Man did just what we feared he'd do. We damned him mightily. And yet, we did not damn him in our hearts. A sailor may be hungry, but he's a sailor still.

The islanders had seen us and were coming off to meet us. Their boats were stacked with fruit. We saw their piles of golden oranges, and yellow bunches of bananas, and heaps of sweet green coconuts all full of luscious milk, and the green leaves of mellow pine-apples. And our Old Man sailed on! We passed the boats so close that we could hear the natives calling, above the sea's high sough, the wind's high pipe. There was a girl in one boat. Paddy threw her a kiss and shouted, " Hey, meet me off the Horn, and warm me up a bit! " And on we flew. And on came that white clipper after us. You don't catch clipper captains halting in a race to let their crews munch fruit! And then we heard the mate say, " Well, I'm damn! They're chucking all the fruit into the water! " And how we damned that tall white clipper then! We raced her two more days, then lost her in a wet wind from the westerly. She'd never gained a foot.

Bill Adams

14

Song

THE BOAT is chafing at our long delay,
   And we must leave too soon
The spicy sea-pinks and the inborne spray,
   The tawny sands, the moon.

Keep us, O Thetis, in our western flight!
   Watch from thy pearly throne
Our vessel, plunging deeper into night
   To reach a land unknown.

John Davidson

A Passer-By

WHITHER, O splendid ship, thy white sails crowding,
   Leaning across the bosom of the urgent West,
That fearest nor sea rising, nor sky clouding,
   Whither away, fair rover, and what thy quest?
   Ah! soon, when Winter has all our vales opprest,
When skies are cold and misty, and hail is hurling,
   Wilt thou glide on the blue Pacific, or rest
In a summer haven asleep, thy white sails furling?

I there before thee, in the country that well thou knowest,
   Already arrived am inhaling the odorous air:
I watch thee enter unerringly where thou goest,
   And anchor queen of the strange shipping there,
   Thy sails for awnings spread, thy masts bare:
Nor is aught from the foaming reef to the snow-capp'd, grandest
   Peak, that is over the feathery palms, more fair
Than thou, so upright, so stately, and still thou standest.

And yet, O splendid ship, unhail'd and nameless,
   I know not if, aiming a fancy, I rightly divine
That thou hast a purpose joyful, a courage blameless,
   Thy port assured in a happier land than mine.

15

But for all I have given thee, beauty enough is thine,
As thou, aslant with trim tackle and shrouding,
From the proud nostril curve of a prow's line
In the offing scatterest foam, thy white sails crowding.

Robert Bridges

A Lonely Sea

A LONELY sea washes the shores of Cyprus. Commerce seems almost to have completely fled the nest in which it first had life. The wanderer who now from the thistle-covered site of Salamis looks eastward to the sunrise, or who casts his glance from the shapeless mounds of Paphos, beholds waves almost as destitute of sail-life as though his stand-point had been taken upon some unmapped island in the South Pacific.

To the north and south this characteristic of loneliness is but little changed. Across the bluest blue waters of the Karamanian Gulf the icy summits of many mountains rise above a shipless horizon, and the beauty of the long indented north shore of Cyprus, from Kyrenia to far-away Cape Andreas, is saddened by the absence of that sense of human existence and of movement which the white speck of canvas bears upon its glistening wing. To the south, commerce is not wholly dead. Between the wide arms of Capes de Gat and Chitti ships and coasting craft are seen at intervals, and the sky-line is sometimes streaked by the long trail of steamer-smoke from some vessel standing in or out of the open roadstead of Larnaca; but even here, although the great highway of the world's commerce is but a day and a half's sail away to the south, man's life upon the waters is scant and transient. But the traveller who stands upon the shores of Cyprus will soon cease to marvel at the absence of life upon the waters outspread before him; the aspect of the land around him, the stones that lie in shapeless heaps at his feet, the bare brown ground upon whose withered bosom sere and rustling thistles alone recall the memory of vegetation—all tell plainly enough the endless story of decay; and, as he turns inwards from a sea which at least has hidden all vestiges of wreck beneath its changeless surface, he sees around him a mouldering tomb, which but half conceals the skeleton of two thousand years of time.

General Sir W. F. Butler

Atlantis

WHAT POETS sang in Atlantis? Who can tell
The epics of Atlantis or their names?
The sea hath its own murmurs, and sounds not
The secrets of its silences beneath,
And knows not any cadences enfolded
When the last bubbles of Atlantis broke
Among the quieting of its heaving floor.

O, years and tides and leagues and all their billows
Can alter not man's knowledge of men's hearts—
While trees and rocks and clouds include our being
We know the epics of Atlantis still:
A hero gave himself to lesser men,
Who first misunderstood and murdered him,
And then misunderstood and worshipped him;
A woman was lovely and men fought for her,
Towns burnt for her, and men put men in bondage,
But she put lengthier bondage on them all;
A wanderer toiled among all the isles
That fleck this turning star of shifting sea,
Or lonely purgatories of the mind,
In longing for his home or his lost love.

Poetry is founded on the hearts of men:
Though in Nirvana or the Heavenly courts
The principle of beauty shall persist,
Its body of poetry, as the body of man,
Is but a terrene form, a terrene use,
That swifter being will not loiter with;
And, when mankind is dead and the world cold,
Poetry's immortality will pass.

Gordon Bottomley

The Long Trail

THERE'S A whisper down the field where the year has shot her yield,
    And the ricks stand grey to the sun,
Singing: " Over then, come over, for the bee has quit the clover,
    And your English summer's done."
        You have heard the beat of the off-shore wind
        And the thresh of the deep-sea rain;
        You have heard the song—how long! how long?
        Pull out on the trail again!
        Ha' done with the Tents of Shem, dear lass,
        We've seen the seasons through,
        And it's time to turn on the old trail, our own trail, the out trail,
        Pull out, pull out, on the Long Trail—the trail that is always new!

It's North you may run to the rime-ringed sun
    Or South to the blind Horn's hate;
Or East all the way into Mississippi Bay,
    Or West to the Golden Gate;
        Where the blindest bluffs hold good, dear lass,
        And the wildest tales are true,
        And the men bulk big on the old trail, our own trail, the out trail,
        And life runs large on the Long Trail—the trail that is always new.

The days are sick and cold, and the skies are grey and old,
    And the twice-breathed airs blow damp;
And I'd sell my tired soul for the bucking beam-sea roll
    Of a black Bilbao tramp;
        With her load-line over her hatch, dear lass,
        And a drunken Dago crew,
        And her nose held down on the old trail, our own trail, the out trail
        From Cadiz Bar on the Long Trail—the trail that is always new.

There be triple ways to take, of the eagle or the snake,
    Or the way of a man with a maid;
But the sweetest way to me is a ship's upon the sea,
    In the heel of the North-East Trade.
        Can you hear the crash on her bows, dear lass,

And the drum of the racing screw,
  As she ships it green on the old trail, our own trail, the out trail,
  As she lifts and 'scends on the Long Trail—the trail that is always
    new?

See the shaking funnels roar, with the Peter at the fore,
  And the fenders grind and heave,
And the derricks clack and grate, as the tackle hooks the crate,
  And the fall-rope whines through the sheave;
    It's " Gang-plank up and in," dear lass,
    It's " Hawsers warp her through! "
    And it's " All clear aft " on the old trail, our own trail, the out trail,
    We're backing down on the Long Trail—the trail that is always
      new.

O the mutter overside, when the port-fog holds us tied,
  And the sirens hoot their dread!
When foot by foot we creep o'er the hueless viewless deep
  To the sob of the questing lead!
    It's down by the Lower Hope, dear lass,
    With the Gunfleet Sands in view,
    Till the Mouse swings green on the old trail, our own trail, the out
      trail,
    And the Gull Light lifts on the Long Trail—the trail that is
      always new.

O the blazing tropic night, when the wake's a welt of light
  That holds the hot sky tame,
And the steady fore-foot snores through the planet-powdered floors
  Where the scared whale flukes in flame!
    Her plates are scarred by the sun, dear lass,
    And her ropes are taut with the dew,
    For we're booming down on the old trail, our own trail, the out
      trail,
    We're sagging south on the Long Trail—the trail that is always
      new.

Then home, get her home, where the drunken rollers comb,
  And the shouting seas drive by,
And the engines stamp and ring, and the wet bows reel and swing,
  And the Southern Cross rides high!

Yes, the old lost stars wheel back, dear lass,
That blaze in the velvet blue.
They're all old friends on the old trail, our own trail, the out trail,
They're God's own guides on the Long Trail—the trail that is
always new.

Fly forward, O my heart, from the Foreland to the Start—
We're steaming all too slow,
And it's twenty thousand mile to our little lazy isle
Where the trumpet-orchids blow!
You have heard the call of the off-shore wind
And the voice of the deep-sea rain;
You have heard the song—how long! how long?
Pull out on the trail again!

The Lord knows what we may find, dear lass,
And The Deuce knows what we may do—
But we're back once more on the old trail, our own trail, the out trail,
We're down, hull down, on the Long Trail—the trail that is always
new!

Rudyard Kipling

Magellan and St. Anselme

MONDAY, the third of October of the said year (1519), at the hour of
midnight, we set sail, making course auster, which the levantine
mariners call Siroc, entering into the ocean sea. We passed the Cape
Verd and the neighbouring islands in fourteen-and-a-half degrees,
and we navigated for several days by the coast of Guinea or Ethiopia;
where there is a mountain called Sierra Leona, which is in eight
degrees latitude according to the art and science of scomography and
astrology. Sometimes we had the wind contrary and at other times
sufficiently good, and rains without wind.

In this manner we navigated with rain for the space of sixty days
until the equinoctial line, which was a thing very strange and un-
accustomed to be seen, according to the saying of some old men and
those who had navigated here several times. Nevertheless, before
reaching this equinoctial line we had in fourteen degrees a variety of
weather and bad winds, as much on account of squalls as for the head
winds and currents which came in such a manner that we could no
longer advance. In order that our ships might not perish nor broach

to (as it often happens when the squalls come together), we struck our sails, and in that manner we went about the sea hither and thither until the fair weather came.

During the calm there came large fishes near the ships which they called *Tiburoni* (sharks), which have teeth of a terrible kind, and eat people when they find them in the sea either alive or dead. These fishes are caught with a device which the mariners call *hamc*, which is a hook of iron. Of these, some were caught by our men. However, they are worth nothing to eat when they are large; and even the small ones are worth but little.

During these storms the body of St. Anselme appeared to us several times; amongst others, one night that it was very dark on account of the bad weather, the said saint appeared in the form of a fire lighted at the summit of the mainmast, and remained there near two hours and a half, which comforted us greatly, for we were in tears, only expecting the hour of perishing; and when that holy light was going away from us it gave out so great a brilliancy in the eyes of each, that we were near a quarter-of-an-hour like people blinded, and calling out for mercy. For without any doubt nobody hoped to escape from that storm.

It is to be noted that all and as many times as that light which represents the said St. Anselme shows itself and descends upon a vessel which is in a storm at sea, that vessel is never lost. Immediately this light had departed the sea grew calmer, and then we saw divers sorts of birds . . .

Fernando Magellan

The Voyage

'TIS A tedious course
By the Antarctic circle: nor beyond
Those sea-wrapt gardens of the dulcet reed,
Bahama and Caribbee, may be found
Safe mole or harbour, till on Falkland's isle
The standard of Britannia shall arise.
Proud Buenos Aires, low-couched Paraguay,
And rough Corrientes, mark, with hostile eye,
The lab'ring vessel: neither may we trust
The dreary naked Patagonian land,
Which darkens in the wind. No traffick there,

No barter for the fleece. There angry storms
Bend their black brows, and, raging, hurl around
Their thunders. Ye advent'rous mariners,
Be firm; take courage from the brave. 'Twas there
Perils and conflicts inexpressible
Anson, with steady undespairing breast,
Endur'd, when o'er the various globe he chas'd
His country's foes. Fast-gath'ring tempests rous'd
Huge ocean, and involv'd him: all around
Whirlwind, and snow, and hail, and horror: now,
Rapidly, with the world of waters, down
Descending to the channels of the deep,
He view'd th' uncover'd bottom of th' abyss;
And now the stars, upon the loftiest point
Toss'd of the sky-mix'd surges. Oft the burst
Of loudest thunder, with the dash of seas,
Tore the wild-flying sails and tumbling masts;
While flames, thick-flashing in the gloom, reveal'd
Ruins of decks and shrouds, and sights of death.

Yet on he far'd, with fortitude his chear,
Gaining, at intervals, slow way beneath
Del Fuego's rugged cliffs, and the white ridge,
Above all height, by op'ning clouds reveal'd,
Of Montegorda, and inaccessible
Wreck-threat'ning Staten-land's o'er-hanging shore,
Enormous rocks on rocks, in ever-wild
Posture of falling; as when Pelion, rear'd
On Ossa, and on Ossa's tott'ring head
Woody Olympus, by the angry gods
Precipitate on earth were doom'd to fall.

At length, through ev'ry tempest, as some branch,
Which from a poplar falls into a loud
Impetuous cataract, though deep immers'd,
Yet reascends, and glides, on lake or stream,
Smooth through the vallies; so his way he won
To the serene Pacific, flood immense,
And rear'd his lofty masts, and spread his sails . . .

John Dyer

On a River Steamer

THE HOUR was the turn of the night, the hour of maximum tension before dawn, the hour when all the world seems plunged in a profundity of slumber whence there can be no awakening, and when the completeness of the silence attunes the soul to special sensibility, and when the stars seem to be hanging strangely close to earth, and the morning star, in particular, to be shining as brightly as a miniature sun. Yet already had the heavens begun to grow coldly grey, to lose their nocturnal softness and warmth, while the rays of the stars were drooping like petals, and the moon, hitherto golden, had turned pale, and become dusted over the silver, and moved further from the earth as intangibly the water of the river sloughed its thick, viscous gleam, and swiftly emitted, and withdrew, stray, pearly reflections of the changes occurring in the heavenly tints.

In the east there was rising, and hanging suspended over the black spears of the pine forest, a thin pink mist the sensuous hue of which was glowing ever brighter, and assuming a density ever greater, and standing forth more boldly and clearly, even as a whisper of timid prayer merges into a song of exultant thankfulness. Another moment, and the spiked tops of the pines blazed into points of red fire resembling festival candles in a sanctuary.

Next, an unseen hand threw over the water, drew along its surface, a transparent and many-coloured net of silk. This was the morning breeze, herald of dawn, as with a coating of tissue-like, silvery scales it rippled the river until the eye grew weary of trying to follow the play of gold and mother-of-pearl and purple and bluish-green reflected from the sun-renovated heavens.

Next, like a fan there unfolded themselves the first sword-shaped beams of day, with their tips blindingly white; while simultaneously one seemed to hear descending from an illimitable height a dense sound-wave of silver bells, a sound-wave advancing triumphantly to greet the sun as his roseate rim became visible over the forest like the rim of a cup that, filled with the essence of life, was about to empty its contents upon the earth, and to pour a bounteous flood of creative puissance upon the marshes whence a reddish vapour as of incense was arising. Meanwhile on the more precipitous of the two banks some of the trees near the river's margin were throwing soft green

23

shadows over the water, while gilt-like dew was sparkling on the herbage, and birds were awakening, and as a white gull skimmed the water's surface on level wings the pale shadow of those wings followed the bird over the tinted expanse, while the sun, suspended in flame behind the forest, like the Imperial bird of the fairy-tale, rose higher and higher into the greenish-blue zenith, until silvery Venus, expiring, herself looked like a bird.

Maxim Gorki

Sea Change

LEAVE NOW the inner land
To walk earth's foot-firm crust,
The heart's worn paths of dust
For smell of weed and sand.

Let these suffice for thought:
White breasts of gulls that turn
Their planing course to burn
In trains of sunset caught,

The cold fingers of foam,
That scuffle up the shore
Swift as the dropped waves roar,
The slant yachts plunging home;

Where red sea-flowers hide
In pools the shingle locks,
Rest by the green-haired rocks,
And watch the yielding tide,

While massive ships that go
Past the downs' ultimate crest,
Wane in the copper West,
And blur, and sink below.

John Lehmann

The Untasted Feast

WIND IS an old wine, comrade:
  A cool, dark wine is rain.
A warm, red wine is sunset:
  Moon wine leaves no stain:
  Drink deeply; ease thy pain.

Clouds are a bread, O comrade,
  A bread for the soul.
Seas are a cool ambrosia,
  Served in a green bowl:
  Eat and be made whole.

Light is a fruit to be picked
  From a tall tree.
It is sweeter than the juice
  Of a wild strawberry:
  Taste, O heart, and see.

The Feast-Table is heavy
  With food of high Heaven.
The Master has called us
  Seventy times seven
  To eat of His leaven.

Seventy times seven
  He has called in vain:
" This is My bread of cloud,
  This is My wine of rain:
  Drink deeply; ease thy pain."

Wilson MacDonald

Emigration

WEAVE O'ER the world your weft, yea weave yourselves,
   Imperial races weave the warp thereof.
   Swift like your shuttle speed the ships, and scoff
At wind and wave. And as a miner delves
For hidden treasure bedded deep in stone,
   So seek ye and find the treasure patriotism
   In lands remote and dipped with alien chrism,
And make those new lands heart-dear and your own.
Weave o'er the world yourselves. Half-human man
   Wanes from before your faces like a cloud
   Sun-stricken, and his soil becomes his shroud.
But of your souls and bodies ye shall make
The sov'reign vesture of its leagueless span,
Clothing with history cliff and wild and lake.

W. M. Rossetti

THE OPEN ROAD

On Going a Journey

ONE OF the pleasantest things in the world is going a journey; but I like to go by myself. I can enjoy society in a room; but out of doors, nature is company enough for me. I am then never less alone than when alone.

> The fields his study, nature was his book.

I cannot see the wit of walking and talking at the same time. When I am in the country I wish to vegetate like the country. I am not for criticizing hedgerows and black cattle. I go out of town in order to forget the town and all that is in it. There are those who for this purpose go to watering-places, and carry the metropolis with them. I like more elbow-room and fewer encumbrances. I like solitude, when I give myself up to it, for the sake of solitude; nor do I ask for

> a friend in my retreat,
> Whom I may whisper solitude is sweet.

The soul of a journey is liberty, perfect liberty, to think, feel, do, just as one pleases. We go a journey chiefly to be free of all impediments and of all inconveniences; to leave ourselves behind, much more to get rid of others. It is because I want a little breathing-space to muse on indifferent matters, where Contemplation

> May plume her feathers and let grow her wings,
> That in the various bustle of resort
> Were all too ruffled, and sometimes impair'd,

that I absent myself from the town for a while, without feeling at a loss the moment I am left by myself. Instead of a friend in a post-chaise or in a Tilbury, to exchange good things with, and vary the same stale topics over again, for once let me have a truce with impertinence. Give me the clear blue sky over my head, and the green turf beneath my feet, a winding road before me, and a three hours' march to dinner—and then to thinking! It is hard if I cannot start some game on these lone heaths. I laugh, I run, I leap, I sing for joy. From the point of yonder rolling cloud I plunge into my past being, and revel there, as the sun-burnt Indian plunges headlong into the wave that wafts him to his native shore. Then long-forgotten things, like " sunken wrack and sumless treasuries", burst upon my eager sight, and I begin to feel, think, and be myself again. Instead of an awkward silence, broken by attempts at wit or dull common-places, mine is that undisturbed silence of the heart which alone is perfect eloquence. No one likes puns, alliterations, antitheses, argument, and analysis better than I do; but I sometimes had rather be without them. " Leave, oh, leave me to my repose! " I have just now other business in hand, which would seem idle to you, but is with me " very stuff o' the conscience ". Is not this wild rose sweet without a comment? Does not this daisy leap to my heart set in its coat of emerald?

William Hazlitt

The Seekers

FRIENDS AND loves we have none, nor wealth nor blessed abode,
But the hope, the burning hope, and the road, the open road.

Not for us are content, and quiet and peace of mind,
For we go seeking cities that we shall never find.

There is no solace on earth for us—for such as we—
Who search for the hidden beauty that eyes may never see.

Only the road and the dawn, the sun, the wind, and the rain,
And the watch-fire under the stars, and sleep, and the road again.

We seek the city of God, and the haunt where beauty dwells,
And we find the noisy mart and the sound of burial bells.

Never the golden city, where radiant people meet,
But the dolorous town where mourners are going about the street.

We travel the dusty road, till the light of the day is dim,
And sunset shows us spires away on the world's rim.

We travel from dawn to dusk, till the day is past and by,
Seeking the holy city beyond the rim of the sky.

Friends and loves we have none, nor wealth nor blessed abode,
But the hope, the burning hope, and the road, the open road.

John Masefield

Country Roads

To COUNTRY people the road is much more than a highway linking distant towns. It is an intimate part of their own lives. It is owned, spiritually, by the people who walk there and dwell by its side. Those who speed along it have no notion of the attachment of the villagers for their road.

The great main roads, which have their own traffic, have had important travellers for two thousand years. The Roman legionaries marched there, later came the Saxon nobles, the Norman knights, the friars, the packmen with strings of ponies, the pilgrims of the Middle Ages. Those broad, metalled roads have always been populous, for they became the coaching roads, and now they are the main motor roads.

The minor roads have always had their own country traffic. The fields that border these ways are known by their Christian names to the men who have worked in them; the woods and streams that fringe the hedges are as familiar as the interior of their own kitchens. In boyhood they played in the water, they hunted for birds' nests in the copses, they explored every corner of the kingdom by their road.

Only the other day an old man told me the names of the fields along his stretch of a Buckinghamshire road. Maria's Field, New Bridge (but the bridge disappeared a hundred years ago when the spring which flowed under it was stopped), Hunt's Lane (where the stag-hunt was held), Brussels, Middle Audeners. He knew the names of the fields for some miles along the country roads, because he had scared birds from the corn in them, he had ploughed there, he had bird-nested in the woods, and minded sheep in the pastures.

So we knew the names of the fields bordering our roads, we knew the names of the horses grazing there, the kinds of trees growing in the hedgerows, the various flowers which came out in their season on the banks, and even the birds that flitted in and out of the bushes. Here grew the first violets, behind the hedge, there the tree-creeper climbed one day, yonder was a bank where we got a wasps'-nest, and we never forgot. These trifles were woven into the road's texture, they became part of it.

A piece of road seemed to belong to us, but overlapping it the next portion would be intimately known by others. So the long winding roads that straggle through England are a part of the life of the people who live by their side. For the country road reveals itself to those who walk often along it, but it keeps its character secret from those who pass without a glance except at the surface of the tar macadam.

The cottage door that opens to the road shares every sight and sound. In fine weather the old people sit there to enjoy the sun and to see all that is going on. They draw their low chairs to the doorway, and bring their sewing, or their newspaper, and they nod and have a word and share their life with others. In Buckinghamshire, the women sit at their doors making exquisite lace, to get the sunshine in their bones and a good light on their work. Travellers are viewed from the discreetly curtained little windows with geraniums on the sill, to keep the outside world from looking within. Nothing is missed by the peering eyes. Little country children are taken for their first outings along the road. When they are old enough they walk up it to school. Some spend their lives near it, but wherever they go out into the world they remember that road, with its hedges, its walls, its trees, as part of their home.

In Burma, in India, in Africa, men can draw on that memory of a road which they know intimately, and they find comfort in thinking of it. So it has happened for generations.

Alison Uttley

The Little Waves of Breffny

THE GRAND road from the mountain goes shining to the sea,
    And there is traffic on it, and many a horse and cart;
But the little roads of Cloonagh are dearer far to me,
    And the little roads of Cloonagh go rambling through my heart.

A great storm from the ocean goes shouting o'er the hill,
    And there is glory in it and terror on the wind;
But the haunted air of twilight is very strange and still,
    And the little winds of twilight are dearer to my mind.

The great waves of the Atlantic sweep storming on their way,
    Shining green and silver with the hidden herring shoal;
But the Little Waves of Breffny have drenched my heart in spray,
    And the Little Waves of Breffny go stumbling through my soul.

Eva Gore Booth

Walking Tours

I<small>T</small> <small>MUST</small> not be imagined that a walking tour, as some would have us fancy, is merely a better or worse way of seeing the country. There are many ways of seeing landscape quite as good; and none more vivid, in spite of canting dilettantes, than from a railway train. But landscape on a walking tour is quite accessory. He who is indeed of the brotherhood does not voyage in quest of the picturesque, but of certain jolly humours—of the hope and spirit with which the march begins at morning, and the peace and spiritual repletion of the evening's rest. He cannot tell whether he puts his knapsack on, or takes it off, with more delight. . . .

Now, to be properly enjoyed, a walking tour should be gone upon alone. If you go in a company, or even in pairs, it is no longer a walking tour in anything but name; it is something else and more in the nature of a picnic. A walking tour should be gone upon alone, because freedom is of the essence; because you should be able to stop and go on, and follow this way or that, as the freak takes you; and because you must have your own pace, and neither trot alongside a champion walker, nor mince in time with a girl. And then you must be open to all impressions and let your thoughts take colour from what you see. You should be as a pipe for any wind to play upon. " I cannot see the wit," says Hazlitt, " of walking and talking at the same time. When I am in the country I wish to vegetate like the country "— which is the gist of all that can be said upon the matter. There should be no cackle of voices at your elbow, to jar on the meditative silence of the morning. And so long as a man is reasoning he cannot surrender himself to that fine intoxication that comes of much motion in the open air, that begins in a sort of dazzle and sluggishness of the brain, and ends in a peace that passes comprehension.

During the first day or so of any tour there are moments of bitterness, when the traveller feels more than coldly towards his knapsack, when he is half in a mind to throw it bodily over the hedge and, like Christian on a similar occasion, " give three leaps and go on singing ". And yet it soon acquires a property of easiness. It becomes magnetic; the spirit of the journey enters into it. And no sooner have you passed the straps over your shoulder than the lees of sleep are cleared from you, you pull yourself together with a shake, and fall at once into your stride. . . .

33

You come to a milestone on a hill, or some place where deep ways meet under trees; and off goes the knapsack, and down you sit to smoke a pipe in the shade. You sink into yourself, and the birds come round and look at you; and your smoke dissipates upon the afternoon under the blue dome of heaven; and the sun lies warm upon your feet, and the cool air visits your neck and turns aside your open shirt. If you are not happy, you must have an evil conscience. You may dally as long as you like by the roadside. It is almost as if the millennium were arrived, when we shall throw our clocks and watches over the housetop, and remember time and seasons no more. Not to keep hours for a lifetime is, I was going to say, to live for ever. You have no idea, unless you have tried it, how endlessly long is a summer's day, that you measure out only by hunger, and bring to an end only when you are drowsy. I know a village where there are hardly any clocks, where no one knows more of the days of the week than by a sort of instinct for the fête on Sundays, and where only one person can tell you the day of the month, and she is generally wrong; and if people were aware how slow Time journeyed in that village, and what armfuls of spare hours he gives, over and above the bargain, to its wise inhabitants, I believe there would be a stampede out of London, Liverpool, Paris, and a variety of large towns, where the clocks lose their heads, and shake the hours out each one faster than the other, as though they were all in a wager. And all these foolish pilgrims would each bring his own misery along with him, in a watch-pocket! . . .

But it is at night, and after dinner, that the best hour comes. There are no such pipes to be smoked as those that follow a good day's march; the flavour of the tobacco is a thing to be remembered, it is so dry and aromatic, so full and so fine. If you wind up the evening with grog, you will own there never was such grog; at every sip a jocund tranquillity spreads about your limbs, and sits easily in your heart. If you read a book—and you will never do so save by fits and starts—you find the language strangely racy and harmonious; words take a new meaning; single sentences possess the ear for half-an-hour together; and the writer endears himself to you, at every page, by the nicest coincidence of sentiment. It seems as if it were a book you had written yourself in a dream. . . .

If the evening be fine and warm, there is nothing better in life than to lounge before the inn door in the sunset, or lean over the parapet of the bridge, to watch the weeds and the quick fishes. It is then, if ever, that you taste joviality to the full significance of that audacious

34

word. Your muscles are so agreeably slack, you feel so clean and so strong and so idle, that whether you move or sit still, whatever you do is done with pride and a kingly sort of pleasure. You fall in talk with any one, wise or foolish, drunk or sober. And it seems as if a hot walk purged you, more than of anything else, of all narrowness and pride, and left curiosity to play its part freely, as in a child or a man of science. You lay aside all your own hobbies, to watch provincial humours develop themselves before you, now as a laughable farce, and now grave and beautiful like an old tale.

Or perhaps you are left to your own company for the night, and surly weather imprisons you by the fire. You may remember how Burns, numbering past pleasures, dwells upon the hours when he has been "happy thinking". It is a phrase that may well perplex a poor modern, girt about on every side by clocks and chimes, and haunted, even at night, by flaming dial-plates. For we are all so busy, and have so many far-off projects to realize, and castles in the fire to turn into solid habitable mansions on a gravel soil, that we can find no time for pleasure trips into the Land of Thought and among the Hills of Vanity. Changed times, indeed, when we must sit all night, beside the fire, with folded hands; and a changed world for most of us, when we find we can pass the hours without discontent, and be happy thinking. We are in such haste to be doing, to be writing, to be gathering gear, to make our voice audible a moment in the derisive silence of eternity, that we forget that one thing, of which these are but the parts—namely, to live. We fall in love, we drink hard, we run to and fro upon the earth like frightened sheep. And now you are to ask yourself if, when all is done, you would not have been better to sit by the fire at home and be happy thinking. . . .

You lean from the window, your last pipe reeking whitely into the darkness, your body full of delicious pains, your mind enthroned in the seventh circle of content; when suddenly the moon changes, the weathercock goes about, and you ask yourself one question more: whether, for the interval, you have been the wisest philosopher or the most egregious of donkeys? Human experience is not yet able to reply; but at least you have had a fine moment, and looked down upon all the kingdoms of the earth. And whether it was wise or foolish, tomorrow's travel will carry you, body and mind, into some different parish of the infinite.

R. L. Stevenson

Alone

FOR I would walk alone,
In storm and tempest, or in starlight nights
Beneath the quiet Heavens; and, at that time,
Have felt whate'er there is of power in sound
To breathe an elevated mood, by form
Or image unprofaned; and I would stand,
Beneath some rock, listening to sounds that are
The ghostly language of the ancient earth,
Or make their dim abode in distant winds.
Thence did I drink the visionary power.
I deem not profitless these fleeting moods
Of shadowy exultation: not for this,
That they are kindred to our purer mind
And intellectual life; but that the soul,
Remembering how she felt, but what she felt
Remembering not, retains an obscure sense
Of possible sublimity, to which,
With growing faculties still growing, feeling still
That whatsoever point they gain, they still
Have something to pursue . . .

William Wordsworth

The Pocket Companion

IN 1722 Thomas Taylor, at the Golden Lyon in Fleet Street, published *The Gentleman's Pocket Companion for Travelling in Foreign Parts*. It was intended rather for the many than "the Wise and Great", and contained descriptions of the roads, distances, maps, and dialogues in English, French, Italian, German and Spanish. How useful the maps were may be judged from the fact that Dijon was not marked. As for the dialogues, the following from a discourse on rising may serve:

"What maiden is that?"

"She is not a maid. She is marry'd."

For asking the way, you might perhaps not need this: "*J'ay eu cinq*

ou six accez de fièvre, qui m'ont fort débilité, et m'ont osté tout l'appétit."[1]
The *Pocket Companion* also offered legal hints, of no very alluring
quality. " If a Stranger pass thro' any Town or Village in the Night,
he may be arrested till Morning; when, if they have no suspicion of
him, he may be dismissed; but if he refuses to obey the Arrest, they
shall levy Hue and Cry after him." Again, " If the Guest be assaulted
and beat within the Inn, he shall have no Action against his Host;
for the Charge of the Host extends to the Moveables only, and not
the Persons of his Guests." Details like that doubtless contributed to
the growth of the Open Road spirit.

Edmund Blunden

Always Back Returning

OFTEN REBUKED, yet always back returning
To those first feelings that were born with me,
And leaving busy chase of wealth and learning
For idle dreams of things which cannot be . . .

I'll walk where my own nature would be leading—
It vexes me to choose another guide—
Where the grey flocks in ferny glades are feeding,
Where the wild wind blows on the mountain-side . . .

Emily Brontë

A Coach-Ride

THERE IS no month in the whole year in which nature wears a more
beautiful appearance than in the month of August. Spring has many
beauties, and May is a fresh and blooming month, but the charms of
this time of year are enhanced by their contrast with the winter season.
August has no such advantage. It comes when we remember nothing
but clear skies, green fields, and sweet-smelling flowers—when the
recollection of snow, and ice, and bleak winds, has faded from our
minds as completely as they have disappeared from the earth—and yet
what a pleasant time it is! Orchards and corn-fields ring with the hum
of labour; trees bend beneath the thick clusters of rich fruit which bow

[1] [" I have had five or six bouts of fever, which made me very weak, and
through which I lost my appetite."]

37

their branches to the ground; and the corn, piled in graceful sheaves, or waving in every light breath that sweeps above it, as if it wooed the sickle, tinges the landscape with a golden hue. . . .

As the coach rolls swiftly past the fields and orchards which skirt the road, groups of women and children, piling the fruit in sieves, or gathering the scattered ears of corn, pause for an instant from their labour, and shading the sun-burned face with a still browner hand, gaze upon the passengers with curious eyes, while some stout urchin, too small to work, but too mischievous to be left at home, scrambles over the side of the basket in which he has been deposited for security, and kicks and screams with delight. The reaper stops in his work, and stands with folded arms, looking at the vehicle as it whirls past; and the rough cart-horses bestow a sleepy glance upon the smart coach team, which says as plainly as a horse's glance can, " It's all very fine to look at, but slow going, over a heavy field, is better than warm work like that, upon a dusty road, after all." You cast a look behind you, as you turn a corner of the road. The women and children have resumed their labour; the reaper once more stoops to his work; the cart-horses have moved on; and all are in motion again.

Charles Dickens

Journey at Night

WE HAD ridden on for some two or three hours; the stir and bustle of our commencing journey had ceased, the liveliness of our little troop had worn off with the declining day, and the night closed in as we entered the great Servian forest. Through this our road was to last for more than a hundred miles. Endless, and endless now on either side, the tall oaks closed in their ranks and stood gloomily lowering over us, as grim as an army of giants with a thousand years' pay in arrear. One strived with listening ear to catch some tidings of the forest world within—some stirring of beasts, some night-bird's scream—but all was quite hushed, except the voice of the cicalas that peopled every bough, and filled the depths of the forest through and through, with one same hum everlasting—more stilling than very silence.

At first our way was in darkness, but after a while the moon got up, and touched the glittering arms and tawny faces of our men with light so pale and mystic, that the watchful Tatar felt bound to look out for demons, and take proper means for keeping them off; forthwith he determined that the duty of frightening away our ghostly enemies (like every other troublesome work) should fall upon the poor Surid-gees, who accordingly lifted up their voices, and burst upon the dreadful stillness of the forest with shrieks and dismal howls. These precautions were kept up incessantly, and were followed by the most complete success, for not one demon came near us, and long before midnight we reached the hamlet in which we were to rest for the night.

A. W. Kinglake

The Lost Road

OF ONE thing I am convinced; that the Scot, even the most hard-headed of his race, is a sentimentalist, a dreamer at heart. Go where he will, he never forgets the clachan or street of his birth.

Sometimes I wonder just how great a part imagination plays in our normal everyday life. In the secret chambers of our minds we conjure up fantasies, live a life so far from our everyday existence, that oft-times it is difficult, when a stray word or picture opens the secret door, to know really if the ghost which appears before our mental eyes was once a material thing or is merely a figment of our dreams. Difficult to explain, but everyone knows such moments.

A sudden glimpse of a patch of willow-herb from the window of an express train, or a crimson tangle of campion in a hedgerow, set me wandering. They take me back to my lost road, a wayside path I have not seen for more years than I care to remember. How strange it seems—my lost road—how foolish it must read to you who know not its genesis nor what to me it stands for! And yet how I love to dream about it at the fireside of an evening, in imagination to sit on the old moss-grown stone of yesteryear and listen to the breeze whisper-ing in the hedgerow.

But my road was not woven of such fanciful stuff. It was real, an actual little byway which led off the hill road, and I can picture it now as I write these words. The deep ruts were made by heavy-laden farm carts, although I never actually saw the grain or the scented hay being brought home to swell the yellow stacks which clustered round the farm steadings. Stray wisps, clinging to the outstretched branches of the wild rose or overhanging arms of an ancient beech, were my only proof. As a rule, I was free to visit the narrow roadway only of an evening, when the farm darg was long ended and the cows had been driven back again to the fields, the last task, milking, finished for another day. . . .

As I say, it is many years ago—too many for the peace of my soul
—that as a boy I used to ramble in this country byway which led to
a cluster of white, straw-thatched cottages. Strange to say, I never
saw anyone either enter or leave those secluded little homes; I never
once met a living person in the winding roadway. . . .

Only the other day an irresistible longing possessed me to visit the
old road again, to find if it had altered with the passing years. But alas!
I could not even find it. The green hill was there, and old Goatfell
still peered across the tumbling waters of the Firth, but now a broad
highway leads to the busy town and my little narrow road has come
under the hand of the improver. Even the white cottages have given
place to a red-tiled bungalow, and a garage stands where the dainty
ferns once nestled on the bank. A little white cottage on a far braeside,
of all the landmarks I then knew, alone remains.

D. C. Cuthbertson

Heat

FROM PLAINS that reel to southward, dim,
The road runs by me white and bare;
Up the steep hill it seems to swim
Beyond, and melt into the glare.
Upward half-way, or it may be
Nearer the summit, slowly steals
A hay-cart, moving dustily
With idly clacking wheels.

By his cart's side the wagoner
Is slouching slowly at his ease,
Half-hidden in the windless blur
Of white dust puffing to his knees.
This wagon on the height above,
From sky to sky on either hand,
Is the sole thing that seems to move
In all the heat-held land.

Beyond me in the fields the sun
Soaks in the grass and hath his will;
I count the marguerites one by one;
Even the buttercups are still.

On the brook yonder not a breath
Disturbs the spider or the midge,
The water-bugs draw close beneath
The cool gloom of the bridge.

Where the far elm-tree shadows flood
Dark patches in the burning grass,
The cows, each with her peaceful cud,
Lie waiting for the heat to pass.
From somewhere on the slope near by
In the pale depth of the noon
A wandering thrush slides leisurely
His thin revolving tune.

In intervals of dreams I hear
The cricket from the droughty ground;
The grasshoppers spin into mine ear
A small innumerable sound.
I lift mine eyes sometimes to gaze:
The woods far off are blue with haze:
The hills are drenched in light.

And yet to me not this or that
Is always sharp or always sweet;
In the sloped shadow of my hat
I lean at rest, and drain the heat;
Nay more, I think some blessed power
Hath brought me wandering idly here:
In the full furnace of this hour
My thoughts grow keen and clear.

Archibald Lampman

Walking

I CAN easily walk ten, fifteen, twenty, any number of miles, commencing at my own door, without going by any house, without
crossing a road except where the fox and the mink do: first along
by the river, and then the brook, and then the meadow and the wood-
side. There are square miles in my vicinity which have no inhabitant.
From many a hill I can see civilization and the abodes of man afar.
The farmers and their works are scarcely more obvious than wood-
chucks and their burrows. Man and his affairs, church and state and
school, trade and commerce, and manufacture and agriculture, even
politics, the most alarming of them all—I am pleased to see how little
space they occupy in the landscape. Politics is but a narrow field, and
that still narrower highway yonder leads to it. I sometimes direct the
traveller thither. If you would go to the political world, follow the
great road—follow that market-man, keep his dust in your eyes, and
it will lead you straight to it; for it, too, has its place merely, and does
not occupy all space. I pass from it as from a beanfield in the forest,
and it is forgotten. In one half-hour I can walk off to some portion
of the earth's surface where a man does not stand from one year's end
to another, and there, consequently, politics are not, for they are but
as the cigar-smoke of man. . . .

I think that I cannot preserve my health and spirits unless I spend
four hours at least, and it is commonly more than that, every day in
the open air; sauntering through the woods and over the hills and
fields, absolutely free from all worldly engagements. You may safely
say, a penny for your thoughts, or a thousand pounds. When sometimes I am reminded that the mechanics and shopkeepers stay in their
shops not only all the forenoon, but all the afternoon too, sitting with
crossed legs, so many of them—as if legs were made to sit upon, and
not to stand or walk upon—I think that they deserve some credit for
not having all committed suicide long ago.

H. D. Thoreau

The Wayside Traveller

IT WAS now dark, and I determined to spend the night in the open, for the air was balmy and the moon made the country look like fairy-land. In the daytime the meadows looked parched, the roads were dusty and the heat was exhausting, but at night on the Hungarian plain there was a delightful, cool breeze and everything in nature seemed to awaken to life. The moonlight shining through the trees carved everything into queer, fantastic shapes. In some places the white light made the foliage look like silver filigree work; in other places the branches became shadowy, ghostly forms.

It is difficult to explain in definite words the sensation of mystery and romance that the wayside traveller finds in Hungary. The scenery seen by the light of day is uninteresting, for the whole country is just a huge plain. But at night in the moonlight the fields of corn, the clumps of trees, the little knolls here and there become meeting-places of fairies. It is the mixture of races that has given to this countryside its poetical charm. To the Magyar mind all that country is inhabited by invisible beings that spring to life when the sun goes down, and I have met peasants who were afraid to wander in the light of the moon for, as they said, the fevers descend on the earth when the moon rides in the sky.

The primitive Magyar is pantheistic in his attitude towards nature and translates this sentiment into the little folk-poems he improvises to the sound of his rustic flute or the Gypsy's fiddle. The Hungarian projects his personality on to his external surroundings. The forest is in mourning because his love lies on her death-bed; Sari has sowed violets and awaits their growing because they symbolize the home-coming of her lover; the shepherd tending his flocks by the Tisza river looks up at the starry sky and thinks of his mother far away in Transylvania or his sister sweeping her room with rosemary boughs.

In the northern countries of Europe the scenery is more majestic than the Hungarian plain, but the peasants do not look on their country through the veil of their own folk-lore or folk-music, nor do they associate each legend and melody with definite events in their country's history to the same extent as the Magyar does. Every step that the lonely traveller makes through the plain is accompanied by songs, dirges and dances until his mind echoes and re-echoes to a mighty symphony composed of countless fragmentary tunes.   *Walter Starkie*

Song of the Open Road

AFOOT AND light-hearted I take to the open road,
Healthy, free, the world before me,
The long brown path before me leading wherever I choose.

Henceforth I ask not good-fortune, I myself am good-fortune,
Henceforth I whimper no more, postpone no more, need nothing,
Done with indoor complaints, libraries, querulous criticisms,
Strong and content I travel the open road.

Walt Whitman

The Watershed
Lines written between Munich and Verona

BLACK MOUNTAINS pricked with pointed pine
  A melancholy sky.
Out-distanced was the German vine,
  The sterile fields lay high.
From swarthy Alps I travelled forth
Aloft; it was the north, the north;
  Bound for the Noon was I.

I seemed to breast the streams that day;
  I met, opposed, withstood
The northward rivers on their way,
  My heart against the flood—
My heart that pressed to rise and reach,
And felt the love of altering speech,
  Of frontiers, in its blood.

But O the unfolding South! the burst
  Of summer! O to see
Of all the southward brooks the first!
  The travelling heart went free
With endless streams; that strife was stopped;
And down a thousand vales I dropped,
  I flowed to Italy.

Alice Meynell

The Monastery at Monte Cassino

AWAY FROM Naples in a glorious sunrise, by the road to Capua, and then on a three days' journey along by-roads, that we may see, on the way, the monastery of Monte Cassino, which is perched on the steep and lofty hill above the little town of San Germano, and is lost on a misty morning in the clouds.

So much the better for the deep sounding of its bell, which, as we go winding up, on mules, towards the convent, is heard mysteriously in the still air, while nothing is seen but the grey mist, moving solemnly and slowly, like a funeral procession. Behold, at length, the shadowy pile of building close before us: its grey walls and towers dimly seen, though so near and so vast: and the raw vapour rolling through its cloisters heavily.

There are two black shadows walking to and fro in the quadrangle, near the statues of the Patron Saint and his sister; and hopping on behind them, in and out of the old arches, is a raven, croaking in answer to the bell, and uttering, at intervals, the purest Tuscan. How like a Jesuit he looks! There never was a sly and stealthy fellow so at home as is this raven, standing now at the refectory door, with his head on one side, and pretending to glance another way, while he is scrutinizing the visitors keenly, and listening with fixed attention. What a dull-headed monk the porter becomes in comparison!

" He speaks like us! " says the porter: " quite as plainly." Quite as plainly, Porter. Nothing could be more expressive than his reception of the peasants who are entering the gate with baskets and burdens. There is a roll in his eye, and a chuckle in his throat, which should qualify him to be chosen Superior of an Order of Ravens. He knows all about it. " It's all right," he says. " We know what we know. Come along, good people. Glad to see you! "

How was this extraordinary structure ever built in such a situation, where the labour of conveying the stone, and iron, and marble so great a height must have been prodigious? " Caw! " says the raven, welcoming the peasants. How, being despoiled by plunder, fire, and earthquake, has it risen from its ruins, and been again made what we now see it, with its church so sumptuous and magnificent? " Caw! " says the raven, welcoming the peasants. These people have a miserable appearance, and (as usual) are densely ignorant, and all beg while

45

the monks are chanting in the chapel. " Caw! " says the raven. " Cuckoo!"

So we leave him chuckling and rolling his eye at the convent gate, and wind slowly down again through the cloud. At last, emerging from it, we come in sight of the village far below, and the flat, green country intersected by rivulets; which is pleasant and fresh to see after the obscurity and haze of the convent—no disrespect to the raven, or the holy friars.

Charles Dickens

LANDSCAPES

A Rare Delight

WHY DOES a virtuous man take delight in landscapes? It is for these reasons: that in a rustic retreat he may nourish his nature; that amid the carefree play of streams and rocks, he may take delight; that he may constantly meet in the country fishermen, woodcutters, and hermits, and see the soaring of the cranes, and hear the crying of the monkeys. The din of the dusty world and the locked-in-ness of human habitations are what human nature habitually abhors; while, on the contrary, haze, mist, and the haunting spirits of the mountains are what human nature seeks, and yet can rarely find.

Shan Shui Hsun

Grongar Hill

EVER CHARMING, ever new,
When will the landskip tire the view!
The fountain's fall, the river's flow,
The woody valleys, warm and low;
The windy summit, wild and high,
Roughly rushing on the sky!
The pleasant seat, the ruined tower,
The naked rock, the shady bower;
The town and village, dome and farm,
Each give each a double charm,
As pearls upon an Æthiop's arm.

See, on the mountain's southern side,
Where the prospect opens wide,
Where the evening gilds the tide;
How close and small the hedges lie!
What streaks of meadows cross the eye!
A step methinks may pass the stream,
So little distant dangers seem;
So we mistake the future's face,
Eyed through hope's deluding glass;
As yon summits soft and fair,
Clad in colours of the air,

Which, to those who journey near,
Barren and brown, and rough appear.
Still we tread tired the same coarse way,
The present's still a cloudy day.

O may I with myself agree,
And never covet what I see;
Content me with an humble shade,
My passions tamed, my wishes laid;
For while our wishes wildly roll,
We banish quiet from the soul:
'Tis thus the busy beat the air,
And misers gather wealth and care.
Now, even now, my joy runs high,
As on the mountain-turf I lie;
While the wanton Zephyr sings,
And in the vale perfumes his wings;
While the waters murmur deep,
While the shepherd charms his sheep;
While the birds unbounded fly,
And with music fill the sky.
Now, even now, my joys run high.

Be full, ye courts; be great who will;
Search for peace, with all your skill:
Open wide the lofty door,
Seek her on the marble floor,
In vain ye search, she is not there;
In vain ye search the domes of care!
Grass and flowers Quiet treads,
On the meads, and mountain-heads,
Along with Pleasure, close allied,
Ever by each other's side:
And often, by the murmuring rill,
Hears the thrush, while all is still,
Within the groves of Grongar Hill.

John Dyer

The Sussex Downs

THOUGH I have now travelled the Sussex downs upwards of thirty years, yet I still investigate that chain of majestic mountains with fresh admiration year by year; and I think I see new beauties every time I traverse it. The range, which runs from Chichester eastward as far as East-Bourn, is about sixty miles in length, and is called The South Downs, properly speaking, only round Lewes. As you pass along, you command a noble view of the wild, or weald, on one hand, and the broad downs and sea on the other. Mr. Ray used to visit a family just at the foot of these hills, and was so ravished with the prospect from Plumpton-plain, near Lewes, that he mentions those scapes in his *Wisdom of God in the Works of the Creation*, with the utmost satisfaction, and thinks them equal to anything he had seen in the finest parts of Europe.

Gilbert White

O the Sweet Valley

O THE sweet valley of deep grass,
Where through the summer stream doth pass,
In chain of shallow, and still pool,
From misty morn to evening cool;
Where the black ivy creeps and twines
O'er the dark-armed, red-trunked pines,
Whence clattering the pigeon flits,
Or, brooding o'er her thin eggs, sits,
And every hollow of the hills
With echoing song the mavis fills.
There by the stream, all unafraid,
Shall stand the happy shepherd maid,
Alone in first of sunlit hours;
Behind her, on the dewy flowers,
Her homespun woollen raiment lies,
And her white limbs and sweet grey eyes
Shine from the calm green pool and deep,
While round about the swallows sweep,
Not silent; and would God that we,
Like them, were landed from the sea.

William Morris

A Vale in Ida

THERE LIES a vale in Ida, lovelier
Than all the valleys of Ionian hills.
The swimming vapour slopes athwart the glen,
Puts forth an arm, and creeps from pine to pine
And loiters, slowly drawn. On either hand
The lawns and meadow-ledges midway down
Stand rich in flowers, and far below them roars
The long brook falling thro' the clov'n ravine
In cataract after cataract to the sea.
Behind the valley topmost Gargarus
Stands up and takes the morning, but in front
The gorges, opening wide apart, reveal
Troas and Ilion's colum'd citadel,
The crown of Troas.

Lord Tennyson

Ku-Ling Pass

WE MARCHED from Kang-K'ou up a narrow valley, wherein the
mules continually stumbled and fell over the great rocks scattered
pell-mell over the path, to a ridge from which we looked down upon
the most extraordinary and confused mass of mountain-tops. Descending again and crossing successive ridges, where, in one of the
valleys, we found some thirty men washing the sand for the very
minute quantity of gold in it, we gained the summit of Ku-Ling
Pass, and, when we put our feet upon the crest, a view so lovely burst
upon us that an exclamation of wonder involuntarily escaped our lips.

Great mountains in front of us, lit up by the setting sun, shone in
all the glory of golden hues, which changed to purple on the lower
slopes, and deepened into blue in the valleys below. This picture was,
as it were, set in a frame by the narrow gorge that ran down from where
we stood, and whose rocky and almost perpendicular sides, rising high
above our heads, presented every variety of colouring. The bluish
grey of the beetling cliffs mingled with the mellow glow of autumn on
the trees, and here and there a touch of delicate green showed some
young saplings just starting into life.

We neither of us could leave the spot, though the hour was late, but stood and watched the changing tints on the mountain-tops. The rosy blush faded from them one by one as the sun fell in the west, little by little the transparent blue in the valley deepened, and the darkening shades stole up the mountain-sides; at length the last flush melted from the highest peak, one star shot its first faint ray of light, and heralding the night reminded us that we must tear ourselves away from the glorious scene. A little temple, perched on the very summit of the northern face, bowered in trees and shrubs, and overlooking the quiet valley, stands in a spot in this season of the year as fair as any on the earth. By the light of the stars that shone with marvellous brilliancy in that cold, clear air, we followed the stream by a rocky path to San-Cha, where we halted after a march of thirty miles.

Captain William Gill

Spring

FROM THE moist meadow to the wither'd hill,
Led by the breeze, the vivid verdure runs;
And swells, and deepens, to the cherish'd eye.
The hawthorn whitens; and the juicy groves
Put forth their buds, unfolding by degrees,
Till the whole leafy forest stands display'd,
In full luxuriance to the sighing gales;
Where the deer rustle thro' the twining brake,
And the birds sing concealed. At once, array'd
In all the colours of the flushing year,
By Nature's swift and secret-working hand,
The garden glows, and fills the liberal air
With lavish fragrance; while the promis'd fruit
Lies yet a little embryo, unperceiv'd,
Within its crimson folds. Now from the town
Buried in smoke, and sleep, and noisome damps,
Oft let me wander o'er the dewy fields,
Where freshness breathes; and dash the trembling drops
From the bent bush, as thro' the verdant maze
Of sweet-briar hedges I pursue my walk;
Or taste the smell of dairy; or ascend
Some eminence, Augusta, in thy plains;
And see the country, far diffus'd around,

One boundless blush; one white-empurpl'd shower
Of mingled blossoms; where the raptur'd eye
Hurries from joy to joy, and hid beneath
The fair profusion, yellow Autumn spies.

James Thomson

The Mountain Road

IT WAS perhaps the wildest view of all my journey. Peak upon peak, chain upon chain of hills ran surging southward, channelled and sculptured by the winter streams, feathered from head to foot with chestnuts, and here and there breaking out into a coronal of cliffs. The sun, which was still far from setting, sent a drift of misty gold across the hill-tops, but the valleys were already plunged in a profound and quiet shadow. . . .

We struck at last into a wide high road carpeted with noiseless dust. The night had come; the moon had been shining for a long while upon the opposite mountain; when on turning a corner my donkey and I issued ourselves into her light. . . .

The road wound and descended swiftly among masses of chestnuts. Hot dust rose from our feet and flowed away. Our two shadows— mine deformed with the knapsack, hers comically bestridden by the pack—now lay before us clearly outlined on the road, and now, as we turned a corner, went off into the ghostly distance, and sailed along the mountain like clouds. From time to time a warm wind rustled down the valley, and set all the chestnuts dangling their bunches of foliage and fruit; the ear was filled with whispering music, and the shadows danced in tune. And next moment the breeze had gone by, and in all the valley nothing moved except our travelling feet.

On the opposite slope, the monstrous ribs and gullies of the mountain were faintly designed in the moonshine; and high overhead, in some lone house, there burned one lighted window, one square spark of red in the huge field of sad nocturnal colouring.

R. L. Stevenson

Nocturne

THE SPLENDOUR falls on castle walls
  And snowy summits old in story:
The long light shakes across the lakes,
  And the wild cataract leaps in glory.
Blow, bugle, blow, set the wild echoes flying,
Blow, bugle; answer, echoes, dying, dying, dying.

  O hark, O hear! how thin and clear,
    And thinner, clearer, farther going!
  O sweet and far from cliff and scar
    The horns of Elfland faintly blowing!
Blow, let us hear the purple glens replying:
Blow, bugle; answer, echoes, dying, dying, dying.

  O love, they die in yon rich sky,
    They faint on hill or field or river:
Our echoes roll from soul to soul,
    And grow for ever and for ever.
Blow, bugle, blow, set the wild echoes flying,
And answer, echoes, answer, dying, dying, dying.

Lord Tennyson

Southern Italy

WE ARE accustomed to hear the south of Italy spoken of as a beautiful country. Its mountain forms are graceful above others, its sea bays exquisite in outline and hue; but it is only beautiful in superficial aspect. In closer detail it is wild and melancholy. Its forests are sombre-leaved, labyrinth-stemmed; the carubbe, the olive, laurel, and ilex, are alike in that strange feverish twisting of their branches, as if in spasms of half-human pain—Avernus forests; one fears to break their boughs, lest they should cry to us from the rents; the rocks they shade are of ashes, or thrice-molten lava; iron sponge whose every pore has been filled with fire. Silent villages, earthquake-shaken, without commerce, without industry, without knowledge, without hope, gleam in white ruin from hillside to hillside; far-winding wrecks of immemorial walls surround the dust of cities long forsaken; the mountain streams moan through the cold arches of their foundations, green with weed, and rage over the heaps of fallen towers. Far above, in thunder-blue serration, stand the eternal edges of the angry Apennines, dark with rolling impendence of volcanic cloud.

John Ruskin

The Sublime

To STAND upon a windy pinnacle,
Beneath the infinite blue of the blue noon,
And underfoot a valley terrible
As that dim gulf, where sense and being swoon
When the soul parts; a giant valley strewn
With giant rocks; asleep, and vast, and still,
And far away. The torrent, which has hewn
His pathway through the entrails of the hill,
Now crawls along the bottom and anon
Lifts up his voice, a muffled tremendous roar,
Borne on the wind an instant, and then gone
Back to the caverns in the middle air;
A voice as of a nation overthrown
With beat of drums, when hosts have marched to war.

Wilfrid Scawen Blunt

The Alps

. . . You ARE in a region over which eternal silence is brooding. Not a sound ever comes there, except the occasional fall of a splintered fragment of rock, or a layer of snow; no stream is heard trickling, and the sounds of animal life are left thousands of feet below. The most that you can hear is some mysterious noise made by the wind eddying round the gigantic rocks; sometimes a strange flapping sound, as if an unearthly flag was shaking its invisible folds in the air. The enormous tract of country over which your view extends —most of it dim and almost dissolved into air by distance—intensifies the strange influence of the silence. You feel the force of the line I have quoted from Wordsworth—

" The sleep that is among the lonely hills."

None of the travellers whom you can see crawling at your feet has the least conception of what is meant by the silent solitudes of the High Alps. To you, it is like a return to the stir of active life, when, after hours of lonely wandering, you return to hear the tinkling of the cow-bells below; to them the same sound is the ultimate limit of the habitable world.

Sir Leslie Stephen

The Ravine

THUS THOU, Ravine of Arve—dark, deep Ravine—
Thou many-coloured, many-voicèd vale,
Over whose pines, and crags, and caverns sail
Fast cloud-shadows and sunbeams: awful scene,
Where Power in likeness of the Arve comes down
From the ice-gulfs that gird his secret throne,
Bursting through these dark mountains like the flame
Of lightning through the tempest; thou dost lie,
Thy giant brood of pines around thee clinging,
Children of elder time, in whose devotion
The chainless winds still come and ever came
To drink their odours, and their mighty swinging
To hear—an old and solemn harmony;
Thine earthly rainbows stretched across the sweep
Of the ethereal waterfall, whose veil
Robes some unsculptured image; the strange sleep
Which when the voices of the desert fail
Wraps all in its own deep eternity;—
Thy caverns echoing to the Arve's commotion,
A loud, lone sound no other sound can tame;
Thou art pervaded with that ceaseless motion,
Thou art the path of the unresting sound—
Dizzy Ravine! and when I gaze on thee
I seem as in a trance sublime and strange
To muse on my own separate fantasy,

My own, my human mind, which passively
Now renders and receives fast influencings,
Holding an unremitting interchange
With the clear universe of things around;
One legion of wild thoughts, whose wandering wings
Now float above thy darkness, and now rest
Where that or thou art no unbidden guest,
In the still cave of the witch Poesy,
Seeking among the shadows that pass by
Ghosts of all things that are, some shade of thee,
Some phantom, some faint image; till the breast
From which they fled recalls them, thou art there!

Percy Bysshe Shelley

Niagara Falls

BEYOND THE foot of the Falls the river is like a slipping floor of marble, green with veins of dirty white, made by the scum that was foam. It slides very quietly and slowly down for a mile or two, sullenly exhausted. Then it turns to a dull sage green, and hurries more swiftly, smooth and ominous. As the walls of the ravine close in, trouble stirs, and the waters boil and eddy. These are the lower rapids, a sight more terrifying than the Falls, because less intelligible. Close in its bands of rock the river surges tumultuously forward, writhing and leaping as if inspired by a demon. It is pressed by the straits into a visibly convex form. Great planes of water slide past. Sometimes it is thrown up into a pinnacle of foam higher than a house, or leaps with incredible speed from the crest of one vast wave to another, along the shining curve between, like the spring of a wild beast. Its motion continually suggests muscular action.

The power manifest in these rapids moves one with a different sense of awe and terror from that of the Falls. Here the inhuman life and strength are spontaneous, active, almost resolute; masculine vigour compared with the passive gigantic power, female, helpless and over-whelming, of the Falls. A place of fear. One is drawn back, strangely, to a contemplation of the Falls, at every hour, and especially by night, when the cloud of spray becomes an immense visible ghost, straining and wavering high above the river, white and pathetic and translucent. The Victorian lies very close below the surface in every man. There one can sit and let great cloudy thoughts of destiny and the passage of empires drift through the mind; for such dreams are at home by Niagara.

I could not get out of my mind the thought of a friend, who said that the rainbows over the Falls were like the arts and beauty and goodness, with regard to the stream of life—caused by it, thrown upon its spray, but unable to stay or direct or affect it, and ceasing when it ceased. In all comparisons that rise in the heart, the river, with its multitudinous waves and its single current, likens itself to a life, whether of an individual or of a community. A man's life is of many flashing moments, and yet one stream; a nation's flows through all its citizens, and yet is more than they. In such places, one is aware, with an almost insupportable and yet comforting certitude, that both men and nations are hurried onwards to their ruin or ending as inevitably as this dark flood. Some go down to it unreluctant, and meet it, like the river, not without nobility. And as incessant, as inevitable, and as unavailing as the spray that hangs over the Falls, is the white cloud of human crying. . . .

With some such thoughts does the platitudinous heart win from the confusion and thunder of Niagara a peace that the quietest plains or most stable hills can never give.

Rupert Brooke

To His Tutor

COME, come away,
And snatch me from these shades to purer day,
 Though Nature lie
Reserv'd, she cannot 'scape thy piercing eye.
 I'll in her bosom stand,
 Led by thy cunning hand,
  And plainly see
  Her treasury;
Though all my light be but a glimpse of thine,
 Yet with that light, I will o'erlook
 Her hardly opened book,
Which to aread is easy, to understand divine.

 Come let us run
And give the world a girdle with the sun;

For so we shall
Take a full view of this enamell'd ball,
  Both where it may be seen
  Clad in a constant green,
      And where it lies
      Crusted with ice;
Where't swells with mountains, and shrinks down to vales;
  Where it permits the usurping sea
    To rove with liberty,
And where it pants with drought, and of all liquor fails. . . .

    Then let's away,
And journey thither: what should cause our stay?
  We'll not be hurl'd
Asleep by drowsy potions of the world.
  Let not Wealth tutor out
  Our spirits with her gout,
    Nor Anger pull
    With cramps the soul;
But fairly disengag'd we'll upward fly,
  Till that occurring joy affright
    Even with its very weight,
And point the haven where we may securely lie.

John Hall

IN TRANSIT

The True Traveller

THE TRUE traveller seeks precisely what the excursionist dreads, and what those who travel with a definite object are indifferent to. It is a sense of escape from all that is homely and habitual—from an earth and a heaven grown sordid with the dust of vain associations. It is the refreshment like that felt by a fevered cheek when a pillow is turned and the touch of the linen is cool again, produced in the mind by new colours on the mountains, new scents in the atmosphere, forests with unknown borders, roads that lead into mystery, castles that rise from the mists of an enchanted past, and men whose aims and characters one cannot despise, not knowing them.

Amongst influences such as these there steals upon the true traveller a delightful sense of being born again to youth. Once more, for the time, he is buoyant with bright illusions, the world is once more fresh to him as it was to the eyes of twenty; life is once more a bubble iridescent with all the colours of hope.

W. H. Mallock

Stepping Westward

" WHAT, you are stepping westward? "—" Yea.
—'Twould be a wildish destiny,
If we, who thus together roam
In a strange land, and far from home,
Were in this place the guests of chance;
Yet who would stop, or fear to advance,
Though home or shelter he had none,
With such a sky to lead him on? "

The dewy ground was dark and cold;
Behind, all gloomy to behold;
And stepping westward seemed to be
A kind of heavenly destiny;
I liked the greeting; 'twas a sound
Of something without place or bound;
And seemed to give me spiritual right
To travel through that region bright.

The voice was soft, and she who spake
Was walking by her native lake;
The salutation had to me
The very sound of courtesy;
Its power was felt; and while my eye
Was fixed upon the glowing sky,
The echo of the voice enwrought
A human sweetness with the thought
Of travelling through the world that lay
Before me in my endless way.

William Wordsworth

Strange Cities

To TRY not to be a tourist is often to be snobbish and to be smug; but it is surely better to risk these dangers than to be satisfied with the stereotyped and expected. What is so tantalizing in a strange city is the sense that it is familiar to its own inhabitants; that a life which seems so impenetrable, so alien to the stranger is in fact habitual to everyone else.

To probe this life as deeply as may be in the time at one's disposal seems to me a chief objective in travel; this, and a readiness to be impressed by the apparently irrelevant. These are questions well understood by those indefatigable English travellers of eighty or ninety years ago, who were not ashamed to be inquisitive nor afraid of being romantic. When they visited Orange they knew that the town pump under the *plantane* tree, or the morning glory on the concierge's lodge, or the way the concierge's grandchild romped in the shadow of the Roman ruins was an essential part of a visit to the *Théâtre Antique*. When they got home they described these things in the tightly-printed, linen-bound books which they published.

They liked to create chance contacts and to try to plumb the depths of a local life. It was this system that, at the risk of being a bore, I was pursuing in this journey to the South, and it is a system which it is easy to work by in the United States, where friendliness is almost universal and strangers are welcomed without the reserve of the English nor the suspicion of the French. I left New Orleans with many kind slow voices echoing in my ears.

" Stay over Tuesday and come to Gulfport."

" But I haven't any more money."

" Oh shucks. I got some money."

" But my leave will be up."

" Shucks. Come to Gulfport. I want you to see Gulfport. *You'd like Gulfport.*"

These last three words sum up, perhaps, one of the ultimate charms of living in America. People want you to do some particular thing for one irresistible reason: because you would like to do it.

James Pope-Hennessy

Ninth-Century India

WHEN A king dies in the island of Serendib, which is the last of the islands of the Indies, his body is laid in an open chariot, in such a posture that his head hangs backward, almost touching the ground, with his hair trailing on the earth; and the chariot is followed by a woman, who sweeps the dust on the face of the deceased, while she proclaims, with a loud voice: " O man! behold your king! He was yesterday your master, but now the dominion which he exercised over you is at an end. He is reduced to the state which you now see, having left the world; and the arbiter of life and death hath withdrawn his soul. Count not, therefore, O man! upon the uncertain hopes of this life." This or a similar proclamation is continued for three days; after which the body is embalmed with sandal-wood, camphor, and saffron, and is then burned, and the ashes are scattered to the winds. . . .

It has often happened in the isle of Serendib, where there is a mine of precious stones in a mountain, a pearl fishery, and other extraordinary things, that an Indian would come into the bazaar or marketplace, armed with a kris, and seize upon the most wealthy merchant there present, leading him out of the market, through a throng of people, holding the kris to his throat, while no one dared to attempt his rescue, as the Indian was sure, in such a case, to kill the merchant and make away with himself; and when he had got the merchant out of the city, the Indian obliged him to redeem his life with a sum of money. To put an end to such outrages an order was issued to seize such trespassers; but on attempting to execute this order, several merchants were killed, both Arabs and Indians, and the order was obliged to be repealed. . . .

An Arab came once to Bassora with a pearl of great value, which he showed to a merchant, and was astonished when he got so large a sum for it as an hundred drams of silver; with which he purchased corn to carry back to his own country. But the merchant carried his acquisition to Bagdad, where he sold it for a large sum of money, by which he afterwards was enabled to extend his dealings to a great amount. The Arab gave the following account of the way in which he had found this large pearl: Going one day along the shore, near Saman, in the district of Bahrein, he saw a fox lying dead, with something hanging at his muzzle which held him fast, which he discovered to be a white lucid shell, in which he found this pearl. He concluded that the oyster had been thrown ashore by a tempest and lay with its shell open on the beach, when the fox, attracted by the smell, had thrust in his muzzle to get at the meat, on which the oyster closed its shell, and held him fast till he died: for it is the property of the oyster never to let go its hold, except forcibly opened, by thrusting in an iron instrument between the shells, carefully guarding its included pearl, as a mother preserves her child.

Trans. Renaudat

The Wanderer

His wandering step
Obedient to high thoughts, has visited
The awful ruins of the days of old:
Athens, and Tyre, and Balbec, and the waste
Where stood Jerusalem, the fallen towers
Of Babylon, the eternal pyramids,
Memphis and Thebes, and whatsoe'er of strange
Sculptured on alabaster obelisk,
Or jasper tomb, or mutilated sphynx,
Dark Æthiopia in her desert hills
Conceals. Among the ruined temples there,
Stupendous columns, and wild images
Of more than man, where marble dæmons watch
The Zodiac's brazen mystery, and dead men
Hang their mute thoughts on the mute walls around,
He lingered, poring on memorials
Of the world's youth, through the long burning day

Gazed on those speechless shapes, nor, when the moon
Filled the mysterious halls with floating shades
Suspended he that task, but ever gazed
And gazed, till meaning on his vacant mind
Flashed like strong inspiration, and he saw
The thrilling secrets of the birth of time.

Percy Bysshe Shelley

Teiresias Advises Odysseus

" MY LORD Odysseus," he began, " you are in search of some easy way
to reach your home. But the powers above are going to make your
journey hard. For I cannot think that you will slip through the hands
of the Earthshaker, who has by no means forgotten his resentment
against you for blinding his beloved son.

" Notwithstanding that, you and your friends may yet reach Ithaca,
though not without mishap, if only you determine to keep a tight hand
on yourself and your men from the moment when your good ship
leaves the deep blue seas and approaches the Isle of Thrinacie, and
you see there at their pasture the cattle and the fat sheep of the Sun-
god, whose eye and ear miss nothing in the world. If you leave them
untouched and fix your mind on getting home, there is some chance
that all of you may yet reach Ithaca, though not in comfort. But if
you hurt them, then I warrant you that your ship and company will
be destroyed, and if you yourself do manage to escape, you will come
home late, in evil plight, upon a foreign ship, with all your comrades
dead.

" You will find trouble too in your house—a set of scoundrels eating
up your stores, making love to your royal consort and offering wedding
gifts. It is true that you will pay out these men for their misdeeds
when you reach home. But whichever way you choose to kill them,
whether by stratagem or in a straight fight with the naked sword, when
you have cleared your palace of these Suitors, you must then set out
once more upon your travels.

" You must take a well-cut oar and go on till you reach a people
who know nothing of the sea and never use salt with their food, so
that our crimson-painted ships and the long oars that serve those ships
as wings are quite beyond their ken. And this will be your cue—a
very clear one, which you cannot miss. When you fall in with some

other traveller who speaks of the 'winnowing-fan' you are carrying on your shoulder, the time will have come for you to plant your shapely oar in the earth and offer Lord Poseidon the rich sacrifice of a ram, a bull, and a breeding-boar. Then go back home and make ceremonial offerings to the immortal gods who live in the broad heavens, to all of them, this time, in due precedence.

" As for your own end, Death will come to you out of the sea, Death in his gentlest guise. When he takes you, you will be worn out after an easy old age and surrounded by a prosperous people. This is the truth that I have told you."

Homer (trans. E. V. Rieu)

O'er Desert Plains

O'ER DESERT plains, and rushy meres,
    And wither'd heaths I rove;
Where tree, nor spire, nor cot appears,
    I pass to meet my love.

But tho' my path were damask'd o'er
    With beauties e'er so fine;
My busy thoughts would fly before,
    To fix alone—on thine.

No fir-crown'd hills cou'd give delight,
    No palace please mine eye:
No pyramid's aerial height,
    Where mouldering monarchs lie.

Unmov'd, should Eastern kings advance,
    Could I the pageant see:
Splendour might catch one scornful glance,
    Not steal one thought from thee.

William Shenstone

Wanderer in Wimbledon

THEN THROUGH the mists of his culture came a hard fact, hard as a pebble. " I walked all the Saturday night," said Leonard. " I walked." A thrill of approval ran through the sisters. But culture closed in again. He asked whether they had ever read E. V. Lucas's *Open Road*.

Said Helen, " No doubt it's another beautiful book, but I'd rather hear about your road."

" Oh, I walked."

" How far? "

" I don't know, nor for how long. It got too dark to see my watch."

" Were you walking alone, may I ask? "

" Yes," he said, straightening himself; " but we'd been talking it over at the office. There's been a lot of talk lately about these things. The fellows there said one steers by the Pole Star, and I looked it up in the celestial atlas, but once out of doors everything gets so mixed——"

" Don't talk to me about the Pole Star," interrupted Helen, who was becoming interested. " I know its little ways. It goes round and round, and you go round after it."

" Well, I lost it entirely. First of all the street lamps, then the trees, and towards morning it got cloudy."

Tibby, who preferred his comedy undiluted, slipped from the room. He knew that this fellow would never attain to poetry, and did not want to hear him trying. Margaret and Helen remained. Their brother influenced them more than they knew: in his absence they were stirred to enthusiasm more easily.

" Where did you start from? " cried Margaret. " Do tell us more."

" I took the Underground to Wimbledon. As I came out of the office I said to myself, ' I must have a walk once in a way. If I don't take this walk now, I shall never take it.' I had a bit of dinner at Wimbledon, and then——"

" But not good country there, is it? "

" It was gas-lamps for hours. Still, I had all the night, and being out was the great thing. I did get into woods, too, presently."

" Yes, go on," said Helen.

" You've no idea how difficult uneven ground is when it's dark."

" Did you actually go off the roads? "

" Oh, yes. I always meant to go off the roads, but the worst of it is that it's more difficult to find one's way."

" Mr. Bast, you're a born adventurer," laughed Margaret. " No professional athlete would have attempted what you've done. It's a wonder your walk didn't end in a broken neck. Whatever did your wife say? "

" Professional athletes never move without lanterns and compasses," said Helen. " Besides, they can't walk. It tires them. Go on."

" I felt like R.L.S. You probably remember how in *Virginibus*——"

" Yes, but the wood. This 'ere wood. How did you get out of it? "

" I managed one wood, and found a road the other side which went a good bit uphill. I rather fancy it was those North Downs, for the road went off into grass, and I got into another wood. That was awful, with gorse bushes, I did wish I'd never come, but suddenly it got light— just while I seemed going under one tree. Then I found a road down to a station, and took the first train I could back to London."

" But was the dawn wonderful? " asked Helen.

With unforgettable sincerity he replied, " No." The word flew again like a pebble from the sling. Down toppled all that had seemed ignoble or literary in his talk, down toppled tiresome R.L.S. and the " love of the earth " and his silk top-hat. In the presence of these women Leonard had arrived, and he spoke with a flow, an exultation, that he had seldom known.

" The dawn was only grey, it was nothing to mention——"

" Just a grey evening turned upside down. I know."

"——and I was too tired to lift up my head to look at it, and so cold too. I'm glad I did it, and yet at the time it bored me more than I can say. And besides—you can believe me or not as you choose—I was very hungry. That dinner at Wimbledon—I meant it to last me all night like other dinners. I never thought that walking would make such a difference. Why, when you're walking you want, as it were, a breakfast and luncheon and tea during the night as well, and I'd nothing but a packet of Woodbines. Lord, I did feel bad! Looking back, it wasn't what you may call enjoyment. It was more a case of sticking to it. I did stick. I—I was determined. Oh, hang it all! what's the good—I mean, the good of living in a room for ever? There one goes on day after day, same old game, same up and down to town, until you forget there is any other game. You ought to see once in a way what's going on outside, if it's only nothing particular after all."

E. M. Forster

Resolution and Independence

THERE WAS a roaring in the wind all night;
The rain came heavily and fell in floods;
But now the sun is rising calm and bright;
The birds are singing in the distant woods;
Over his own sweet voice the Stock-dove broods;
The Jay makes answer as the Magpie chatters;
And all the air is filled with pleasant noise of waters.

All things that love the sun are out of doors;
The sky rejoices in the morning's birth;
The grass is bright with rain-drops;—on the moors
The hare is running races in her mirth;
And with her feet she from the plashy earth
Raises a mist; that, glittering in the sun,
Runs with her all the way, wherever she doth run.

I was a Traveller then upon the moor;
I saw the hare that raced about with joy;
I heard the woods and distant waters roar;
Or heard them not, as happy as a boy:
The pleasant season did my heart employ:
My old remembrances went from me wholly;
And all the ways of men, so vain and melancholy.

William Wordsworth

The Winter Sun

BUT SO have I seen the sun kiss the frozen earth, which was bound up with the images of death and the colder breath of the North; and then the waters break from their enclosures, and melt with joy, and run in useful channels; and the flies do rise again from their little graves in walls, and dance awhile in the air, to tell that there is joy within, and that the great mother of creatures will open the stock of her new refreshment, become useful to mankind, and sing praises to her Redeemer.

Jeremy Taylor

71

Young Travellers

FROM SCHOOL to Cam or Isis, and thence home;
And thence with all convenient speed to Rome.
With reverend tutor clad in habit lay,
To tease for cash, and quarrel with all day;
With memorandum-book for every town,
And every post, and where the chaise broke down;
His stock a few French phrases got by heart,
With much to learn, but nothing to impart;
The youth, obedient to his sire's commands,
Sets off a wanderer into foreign lands,
Surprised at all they meet, the gosling pair,
With awkward gait, stretch'd neck, and silly stare,
Discover huge cathedrals built in stone,
And steeples towering high much like our own;
But show peculiar light by many a grin
At popish practices observed within.
    Ere long some bowing, smirking, smart *abbé*
Remarks two loiterers that have lost their way;
And, being always primed with *politesse*
For men of their appearance and address,
With much compassion undertakes the task,
To tell them more than they have wit to ask:
Points to inscriptions wheresoe'er they tread,
Such as, when legible, were never read,
But, being canker'd now and half worn out,
Craze antiquarian brains with endless doubt;
Some headless hero, or some Caesar, shows—
Defective only in his Roman nose;
Exhibits elevations, drawings, plans;
Models of Herculean pots and pans;
And sells them medals, which if neither rare
Nor ancient, will be so, preserved with care.
    Strange the recital! from whatever cause
His great improvement and new light he draws,
The squire, once bashful, is shamefaced no more,
But teems with powers he never felt before;

Whether increased momentum, and the force
With which from clime to clime he sped his course
(As axles sometimes kindle as they go)
Chafed him, and brought dull nature to a glow;
Or whether clearer skies and softer air,
That made Italian flowers so sweet and fair,
Freshening his lazy spirits as he ran,
Unfolded genially and spread the man;
Returning he proclaims by many a grace,
By shrugs and strange contortions of his face,
How much a dunce, that has been sent to roam,
Excels a dunce, that has been kept at home.

William Cowper

The Stage Coach

PERHAPS IT might be owing to the pleasing serenity that reigned in my own mind, that I fancied I saw cheerfulness in every countenance throughout the journey. A stage coach, however, carries animation always with it, and puts the world in motion as it whirls along. The horn, sounded at the entrance of a village, produces a general bustle. Some hasten forth to meet friends; some with bundles and bandboxes to secure places, and in the hurry of the moment can hardly take leave of the group that accompanies them.

In the meantime the coachman has a world of small commissions to execute. Sometimes he delivers a hare or pheasant; sometimes jerks a small parcel or newspaper to the door of a public-house; and sometimes, with knowing leer and words of sly import, hands to some half-blushing, half-laughing housemaid an odd-shaped *billet doux* from some rustic admirer. As the coach rattles through the village, everyone runs to the window, and you have glances on every side of fresh country faces and blooming giggling girls. At the corners are assembled juntos of village idlers and wise men, who take their stations there for the important purpose of·seeing company pass; but the sagest knot is generally at the blacksmith's, to whom the passing of the coach is an event fruitful of much speculation.

Washington Irving

Enchanted Ground

WE WERE at the foot of the American Fall. I could see an immense torrent of water tearing headlong down from some great height, but had no idea of shape, or situation, or anything but vague immensity.

When we were seated in the little ferry-boat, and were crossing the swollen river immediately before both cataracts, I began to feel what it was: but I was in a manner stunned, and unable to comprehend the vastness of the scene. It was not until I came on Table Rock, and looked—Great Heaven, on what a fall of bright green water!—that it came upon me in its full might and majesty.

Then, when I felt how near to my Creator I was standing, the first effect, and the enduring one—instant and lasting—of the tremendous spectacle, was Peace. Peace of Mind, tranquillity, calm recollections of the Dead, great thoughts of Eternal Rest and Happiness: nothing of gloom or terror. Niagara was at once stamped upon my heart, an Image of Beauty; to remain there, changeless and indelible, until its pulses cease to beat, for ever.

Oh, how the strife and trouble of daily life receded from my view, and lessened in the distance, during the ten memorable days we passed on that Enchanted Ground! What voices spoke from out the thundering water; what faces, faded from the earth, looked out upon me from its gleaming depths; what Heavenly promise glistened in those angels' tears, the drops of many hues, that showered around, and twined themselves about the gorgeous arches which the changing rainbows made!

I never stirred in all that time from the Canadian side, whither I had gone at first. I never crossed the river again; for I knew there were people on the other shore, and in such a place it is natural to shun strange company. To wander to and fro all day, and see the cataracts from all points of view; to stand upon the edge of the Great Horseshoe Fall, marking the hurried water gathering strength as it approached the verge, yet seeming, too, to pause before it shot into the gulf below; to gaze from the river's level up at the torrent as it came streaming down; to climb the neighbouring heights and watch it through the trees, and see the wreathing water in the rapids hurrying on to take its fearful plunge; to linger in the shadow of the solemn rock three miles below; watching the river as, stirred by no visible cause, it heaved and eddied and awoke the echoes, being troubled yet, far down beneath the surface, by its giant leap; to have Niagara before me lighted by the sun and by the moon, red in the day's decline, and grey as evening slowly fell upon it; to look upon it every day, and wake up in the night and hear its ceaseless voice: this was enough.

I think in every quiet season now, still do those waters roll and leap, and roar and tumble, all day long; still are the rainbows spanning them, a hundred feet below. Still, when the sun is on them, do they shine and glow like molten gold. Still, when the day is gloomy, do they fall like snow, or seem to crumble away like the front of a great chalk cliff, or roll down the rock like dense white smoke. But always does the mighty stream appear to die as it comes down, and always from its unfathomable grave arises that tremendous ghost of spray and mist, which is never laid: which has haunted this place with the same dread solemnity since Darkness brooded on the deep, and that first flood before the Deluge—Light—came rushing on Creation at the word of God.

Charles Dickens

The Listeners

" Is THERE anybody there?" said the Traveller,
  Knocking on the moonlit door;
And his horse in the silence champed the grasses
  Of the forest's ferny floor:
And a bird flew up out of the turret,
  Above the Traveller's head:
And he smote upon the door again a second time;
  " Is there anybody there?" he said.
But no one descended to the Traveller;
  No head from the leaf-fringed sill
Leaned over and looked into his grey eyes,
  Where he stood perplexed and still.
But only a host of phantom listeners
  That dwelt in the lone house then
Stood listening in the quiet of the moonlight
  To that voice from the world of men:
Stood thronging the faint moonbeams on the dark stair,
  That goes down to the empty hall,
Hearkening in an air stirred and shaken
  By the lonely Traveller's call.

And he felt in his heart their strangeness,
  Their stillness answering his cry,
While his horse moved, cropping the dark turf,
  'Neath the starred and leafy sky;
For he suddenly smote on the door, even
  Louder, and lifted his head:—
" Tell them I came, and no one answered,
  That I kept my word! " he said.
Never the least stir made the listeners,
  Though every word he spake
Fell echoing through the shadowiness of the still house
  From the one man left awake;
Ay, they heard his foot upon the stirrup,
  And the sound of iron on stone,
And how the silence surged softly backward,
  When the plunging hoofs were gone.

Walter de la Mare

Camp for the Night

MY MOST successful Dutch-oven rolls were prepared in the middle of the St. John's River. The doctor and his wife Dessie and I were on a fishing trip on a warm winter day down the Ocklawaha River to its junction with the St. John's, through little Lake George, to the mouth of Salt Springs Run, where we planned to cook supper and camp for the night. I had brought along my large Dutch oven and a big bowl of dough for my rolls. We fished late into the afternoon, and it was plain that by the time we reached our camping place, it would be too late to set my dough to rise. There would be time enough for the baking, for the fish must be cleaned and fried.

We estimated the time to the landing, and an hour and a quarter beforehand, I brought out my bowl of dough, my extra flour, my butter and my Dutch oven from under a seat of the row-boat, and while spray from the wind-swept river dashed into my face, I mixed the dough in the bowl in my lap, shaped my rolls and placed them tenderly in the Dutch oven. I put the oven far forward where the late afternoon sun would rest on the lid, and by the time we reached Salt Springs Run and the camp fire was built, the rolls had risen and were ready for the baking. They had never been so delicious. Supper was superb, the fresh-caught bass white and sweet and firm, the coffee strong and good as it can only be in the open.

We were on a little promontory at the mouth of the run, with great live oaks around us, and palms tall against the aquamarine evening sky. A full moon rose in front of us and we felt ourselves favoured of all mortals. After so much delight we might have expected to pay the piper. The night was hideous. Because the time was winter, we had assumed there would be no mosquitoes. But because the winter was warm, they had hatched, and as we lay on blankets on the sand they descended in swarms. We built up the camp fire to make smoke to drive them away and the smoke was more annoying than the mosquitoes. Hoot owls settled in the oaks over our heads and cried jeeringly all night. Wood roaches came in and awakened us from our spasms of slumber with their sharp nibbling on our ears. When we arose at dawn, the doctor said, " You know, the only thing that kept me going through the night was remembering those rolls."

Marjorie Kinnan Rawlings

Over the Timor Sea

DAYBREAK FOUND us high over the Timor Sea, heading through a world of battleship-grey for Koepang on the Island of Timor, 518 miles distant. On a long finger of land near Darwin, the Point Charles light winked a red eye in a sleeping world—it was our last link with the Fifth Continent.

Ahead, a full moon, white and luminous, was set in our course and behind us the crimson ball of the sun was peeping over the eastern horizon. Soon the orange dawn rolled up like a marching host with chariots and horsemen; up there, 10,000 feet in another world, you could almost hear the fanfare of trumpets as, before the onrushing banners of a new day, the vanquished moon waned and reluctantly disappeared.

Ere long we saw the water far below, dead and lustreless, until full dawn spilled its warmth and brilliance over the tropic sea. Across the lonely sheet of water, bereft of landmarks and unusually devoid of shipping, many an aviator from the Old World had stared with anxious eyes, seeking Darwin; some had missed it and had landed in distress far along the inhospitable and practically uninhabited northern coast of Australia.

Later, we discerned a small lugger, one of those gipsies of these northern waters which nose their lonely way round Australia's tropical coast and across to the Isles of the Indies. That speck on the sea gave us a comforting feeling, for it was suggestive of life as we raced on through an inanimate world.

Charles H. Holmes

Letter from Turkey

I WAS invited to dine with the Grand-Vizier's lady, and it was with a great deal of pleasure I prepared myself for an entertainment which was never before given to any Christian. I thought I should very little satisfy her curiosity (which I did not doubt was a considerable motive to the invitation) by going in a dress she was used to see, and therefore dressed myself in a court habit of Vienna, which is much more magnificent than ours. However, I chose to go *incognito*, to avoid any disputes about ceremony, and went in a Turkish coach, only attended by my woman that held up my train, and the Greek lady who was my interpretess.

I was met at the court door by her black eunuch, who helped me out of the coach with great respect, and conducted me through several rooms, where her she-slaves, finely dressed, were ranged on each side. In the innermost I found the lady sitting on her sofa, in a sable vest. She advanced to meet me, and presented me half a dozen of her friends with great civility. She seemed a good-looking woman, near fifty years old. I was surprised to observe so little magnificence in her house, the furniture being all very moderate; and, except the habits and numbers of her slaves, nothing about her appeared expensive. She guessed at my thoughts, and told me she was no longer of an age to spend either her time or money in superfluities; that her whole expense was charity, and her whole employment praying to God. There was no affectation in this speech; both she and her husband are entirely given up to devotion. He never looks upon any other woman; and, what is much more extraordinary, touches no bribes, notwithstanding the example of all his predecessors. . . .

She entertained me with all kind of civility till dinner came in, which was served, one dish at a time, to a vast number, all finely dressed after their manner, which I don't think so bad as you have perhaps heard it represented. I am a very good judge of their eating, having lived three weeks in the house of an *effendi* at Belgrade, who gave us magnificent dinners, dressed by his own cooks. The first week they pleased me extremely; but I own I then began to grow weary of their table, and desired our own cook might add a dish or two after our manner. But I attribute this to custom, and am very much inclined to believe that an Indian, who had never tasted of either, would prefer their cookery to ours. Their sauces are very high, all the roast very much done. They use a great deal of very rich spice. The soup is served for the last dish; and they have at least as great a variety of ragouts as we have. I was very sorry I could not eat of as many as the good lady would have had me, who was very earnest in serving me of everything. The treat concluded with coffee and perfumes, which is a high mark of respect; two slaves kneeling *censed* my hair, clothes, and handkerchief. After this ceremony, she commanded her slaves to play and dance, which they did with their guitars in their hands, and she excused to me their want of skill, saying she took no care to accomplish them in the art.

Lady Mary Wortley Montagu

The Face of the Desert

GOING UP the Nile is like running the gauntlet before Eternity. Till one has seen it, one does not realize the amazing thinness of that little damp trickle of life that steals along undefeated through the jaws of established death. A rifle-shot would cover the widest limits of cultivation, a bow-shot would reach the narrower. Once beyond them a man may carry his next drink with him till he reaches Cape Blanco on the west (where he may signal for one from a passing Union Castle boat) or the Karachi Club on the east. Say four thousand dry miles to the left hand and three thousand to the right.

The weight of the Desert is on one, every day and every hour. At morning, when the cavalcade tramps along in the rear of the tulip-like dragoman, She says: " I am here—just beyond that ridge of pink sand that you are admiring. Come along, pretty gentleman, and I'll tell your fortune." But the dragoman says very clearly: " Please, sar, do not separate yourself at *all* from the main body," which, the Desert knows well, you had no thought of doing. At noon, when the stewards rummage out lunchtime drinks from the dewy ice-chest, the Desert whines louder than the well-wheels on the bank: " I am here, only a

79

quarter of a mile away. For mercy's sake, pretty gentleman, spare a mouthful of that prickly whisky-and-soda you are lifting to your lips. There's a white man a few hundred miles off, dying on my lap of thirst—thirst that you cure with a rag dipped in luke-warm water while you hold him down with one hand, and he thinks he is cursing you aloud, but he isn't, because his tongue is outside his mouth and he can't get it back. Thank *you*, my noble captain!" For naturally one tips half the drink over the rail with the ancient prayer: " May it reach him who needs it ", and turns one's back on the pulsing ridges and fluid horizons that are beginning their mid-day mirage-dance.

At evening the Desert obtrudes again—tricked out as a Nautch girl in veils of purple, saffron, gold-tinsel, and grass-green. She postures shamelessly before the delighted tourists with woven skeins of home-ward-flying pelicans, fringes of wild duck, black spotted on crimson, and cheap jewellery of opal clouds. " Notice Me!" She cries, like any other worthless woman. "Admire the play of My mobile features— the revelations of My multi-coloured soul! Observe My allurements and potentialities. Thrill while I stir you!" So She floats through all Her changes and retires upstage into the arms of dusk. But at mid-night She drops all pretence and bears down in Her natural shape, which depends upon the conscience of the beholder and his distance from the next white man.

Rudyard Kipling

Lure of Rivers

RIVERS MUST have been the guides which conducted the footsteps of the first travellers. They are the constant lure, when they flow by our doors, to distant enterprise and adventure; and, by a natural impulse, the dwellers on the banks will at length accompany their currents to the low-lands of the globe, or explore at their invitation the interior of conti-nents. They are the natural highways of all nations, not only levelling the ground and removing obstacles from the path of the traveller, quenching his thirst and bearing him on their bosoms, but conducting him through the most interesting scenery, the most populous portions of the globe, and where the animal and vegetable kingdoms attain their greatest perfection.

H. D. Thoreau

The Nile

IT FLOWS through old hushed Egypt and its sands,
  Like some grave mighty thought threading a dream,
  And times and things, as in that vision, seem
Keeping along it their eternal stands,—
Caves, pillars, pyramids, the shepherd bands
  That roamed through the young world, the glory extreme
  Of high Sesostris, and that southern beam,
The laughing queen that caught the world's great hands.

Then comes a mightier silence, stern and strong,
As of a world left empty of its throng,
  And the void weighs on us; and then we wake,
And hear the fruitful stream lapsing along
  'Twixt villages, and think how we shall take
  Our own calm journey on for human sake.

Leigh Hunt

Winter in the Antarctic

" WE SAID good-bye to the sun on May 1 and entered the period of twilight that would be followed by the darkness of mid-winter. The sun by the aid of refraction just cleared the horizon at noon and set shortly before 2 p.m. A fine aurora in the evening was dimmed by the full moon, which had risen on April 27 and would not set again until May 6. The disappearance of the sun is apt to be a depressing event in the polar regions, where the long months of darkness involve mental as well as physical strain. But the *Endurance*'s company refused to abandon their customary cheerfulness, and a concert in the evening made the Ritz, as we called the 'tween decks, where we now lived, a scene of noisy merriment.

" One feels our helplessness as the long winter night closes upon us. By this time, if fortune had smiled upon the Expedition, we would have been comfortably and securely established in a shore base, with depots laid to the south and plans made for the long march in the spring and summer. Where will we make a landing now? It is not easy to forecast the future. The ice may open in the spring, but by that time we will be far to the north-west. I do not think we shall be able to work back to Vahsel Bay. There are possible landing-places on the western coast of the Weddell Sea, but can we reach any suitable spot early enough to attempt the overland journey next year? Time alone will tell. I do not think any member of the Expedition is disheartened by our disappointment. All hands are cheery and busy, and will do their best when the time for action comes. In the meantime we must wait."

Sir Ernest Shackleton

PEOPLE

THIS BRINGS me to my point; and naturally leads me (if the see-saw of this *Désobligeant* will but let me get on) into the efficient as well as final causes of travelling—

Your idle people that leave their native country, and go abroad for some reason or reasons which may be derived from one of these general causes—

Infirmity of body,
Imbecility of the mind, or
Inevitable necessity.

The first two include all those who travel by land or by water, labouring with pride, curiosity, vanity, or spleen, subdivided and combined *in infinitum.*

The third class includes the whole army of peregrine martyrs; more especially those travellers who set out upon their travels with the benefit of the clergy, either as delinquents travelling under the direction of governors recommended by the magistrate—or young gentlemen transported by the cruelty of parents and guardians, and travelling under the direction of governors recommended by Oxford, Aberdeen, and Glasgow.

There is a fourth class, but their number is so small, that they would not deserve a distinction, was it not necessary in a work of this nature to observe the greatest precision and nicety, to avoid a confusion of character. And these men I speak of, are such as cross the seas and sojourn in a land of strangers, with a view of saving money for various reasons and upon various pretences: but as they might also save themselves and others a great deal of unnecessary trouble by saving their money at home—and as their reasons for travelling are the least complex of any other species of emigrants, I shall distinguish these gentlemen by the name of

Simple Travellers.

Thus the whole circle of travellers may be reduced to the following *heads*:

Idle Travellers,
Inquisitive Travellers,

Lying Travellers,
Proud Travellers,
Vain Travellers,
Splenetic Travellers.

Then follow

The Travellers of Necessity,
The Delinquent and Felonious Traveller,
The Unfortunate and Innocent Traveller,
The Simple Traveller.

And last of all (if you please) the Sentimental Traveller (meaning thereby myself). . . .

Laurence Sterne

Parisians

JOSTLE YOUR way as rapidly as may be out of the Rue Vavin, cross the Rue d'Assas, and pass through the little corner gate into the Luxembourg Gardens. What a breath of young grass and hawthorn in blossom to replace the oniony whiff of the third-rate restaurant, the pent staleness of the narrow street! This is the freshest and most pastoral corner of the gardens, where large trees lean down to touch the grass, unvexed by lopping or strict relation to their neighbours, where a hamlet of beehives has a grove to itself, and there are no flower-beds. But it is not popular; only the sourest of the *bonnes*, the most select of the children, the moodiest of the idlers, take their pleasure here among the horse-chestnuts and copper beeches; even the dogs know it to be a mere health resort, and mope obediently along upon their leashes with a demeanour shorn of gallantry.

It is at the other side of the gardens, where prim alleys of young trees spring geometrically from acres of gravel, and the merry-go-round circles everlastingly to a muffled internal tune, that the world of fashion is to be found. There are many seats among the thin tree-stems, and each groans beneath its load of nurses, babies, and underlings of the nurse; family parties sit in circles on hired chairs, conversing with amazing zest round perambulators, both double and single; little girls ply their skipping-ropes like clockwork. Here it is that French domestic life, long maligned, shows itself in colours as gratifying as unexpected, transcending our vaunted English variety.

86

It is not only that the father of the family tolerates his offspring in a public and cheerful manner, a condescension which we esteem almost touching; here, unwearied, he whirls the skipping-rope for the skipping of his yellow-faced daughters, he conciliates the baby in its most apoplectic paroxysm of spleen, he holds long and beautifully histrionic conversations with his mother-in-law and his great-aunt by marriage. He is a pattern even to Mr. Fairchild, who, to the best of my re-collection, was in the habit of " stretching himself on the grass, at a little distance, with his book ", when his children had tea and anecdotes out-of-doors. Even from this paragon among parents Mrs. Sherwood expected no more.

E. Œ. Somerville and Martin Ross

An Italian in America, 1524

TOUCHING THE religion of this people which we have found, for want of their language we could not understand neither by signs nor gesture that they had any religion or law at all, or that they did acknowledge any first cause or mover, neither that they worship the heaven or stars, the sun or moon or other planets, and much less whether they be idolaters, neither could we learn whether that they used any kind of sacrifices or other adorations; neither in their villages have they any temples or houses of prayer. We suppose that they have no religion at all, and that they live at their own liberty. And that all this proceedeth of ignorance, for that they are very easy to be persuaded: and all that they see us Christians do in our divine service, they did the same with the like imitation as they saw us to do it.

John Verrazzano

A Briton in Holland, 1754

YOU MAY expect some account of this country, and though I am not as yet well qualified for such an undertaking, yet shall I endeavour to satisfy some part of your expectations. Nothing surprises me more than the books every day published, descriptive of the manners of this country.

Any young man who takes it into his head to publish his travels, visits the countries he intends to describe; passes through them with as much inattention as his *valet de chambre*; and consequently not having a fund himself to fill a volume, he applies to those who wrote before him, and gives us the manners of a country, not as he must have seen them, but such as they might have been fifty years before. The modern Dutchman is quite a different creature from him of former times; he in everything imitates a Frenchman but in his easy dis-engaged air, which is the result of keeping polite company. The Dutchman is vastly ceremonious, and is perhaps exactly what a Frenchman might have been in the reign of Louis XIV. Such are the better-bred. But the downright Hollander is one of the oddest figures in nature. Upon a head of lank hair he wears a half-cocked narrow leaved hat laced with black ribbon: no coat, but seven waistcoats, and nine pairs of breeches; so that his hips reach almost up to his armpits. This well-clothed vegetable is now fit to see company, or make love. But what a pleasing creature is the object of his appetite? Why, she wears a large frieze cap with a deal of Flanders lace: and for every pair of breeches he carries, she puts on two petticoats. . . .

A Dutch lady burns nothing about her phlegmatic admirer but his tobacco. You must know, Sir, every woman carries in her hand a stove with coals in it, which, when she sits, she snugs under her petti-coats; and at this chimney dozing Strephon lights his pipe. I take it that this continual smoking is what gives the man the ruddy healthful complexion he generally wears, by draining his superfluous moisture, while the woman, deprived of this amusement, overflows with such viscidities as taint the complexion, and give that paleness of visage which low fenny grounds and moist air conspire to cause. A Dutch woman and Scotch will well bear opposition.

The one is pale and fat, the other lean and ruddy: the one walks as if she were straddling after a go-cart, and the other takes too masculine a stride. I shall not endeavour to deprive either country of its share of beauty; but must say, that of [all] objects on this earth, an English farmer's daughter is most charming. Every woman there is a complete beauty, while the higher class of women want many of the requisites to make them even tolerable.

Their pleasures here are very dull, though very various. You may smoke, you may doze; you may go to the Italian comedy, as good an amusement as either of the former. This entertainment always brings in Harlequin, who is generally a magician, and in consequence of his diabolical art performs a thousand tricks on the rest of the persons of the drama, who are all fools. I have seen the pit in a roar of laughter at his humour, when with his sword he touches the glass which another was drinking from. 'Twas not his face they laughed at, for that was masked. They must have seen something vastly queer in the wooden sword, that neither I, nor you, Sir, were you there, could see.

In winter, when their canals are frozen, every house is forsaken, and all people are on the ice; sleds, drawn by horses, and skating, are at that time the reigning amusements. They have boats here that slide on the ice, and are driven by the winds. When they spread all their sails, they go more than a mile and a half a minute. Their motion is so rapid the eye can scarce accompany them. Their ordinary manner of travelling is very cheap, and very convenient: they sail in covered boats drawn by horses; and in these you are sure to meet people of all nations. Here the Dutch slumber, the French chatter, and the English play cards. Any man who likes company may have them to his taste. For my part I generally detached myself from all society, and was wholly taken up in observing the face of the country. Nothing can equal its beauty; wherever I turn my eye, fine houses, elegant gardens, statues, grottos, vistas, present themselves; but enter their towns and you are charmed beyond description. Nothing can be more clean or beautiful.

Oliver Goldsmith

The English

THAT ISLAND of England breeds very valiant creatures: their mastiffs are of unmatchable courage . . . and the men do sympathize with the mastiffs in robustious and rough coming on, leaving their wits with their wives: and then give them great meals of beef and iron and steel, they will eat like wolves and fight like devils.

William Shakespeare

London, 1827

I HAVE seen the greatest wonder which the world can show to the astonished spirit; I have seen it, and am more astonished than ever—and still there remains fixed in my memory that stone forest of houses, and amid them the rushing stream of faces, of living human faces, with all their motley passions, all their terrible impulses of love, of hunger, and of hate—I am speaking of London.

Send a philosopher to London, but no poet! Send a philosopher there, and stand him at a corner of Cheapside, he will learn more there than from all the books of the last Leipzig fair; and as the human waves roar around him, so will a sea of new thoughts rise before him, and the Eternal Spirit which moves upon the face of the waters will breathe upon him; the most hidden secrets of social harmony will be suddenly revealed to him, he will hear the pulse of the world beat audibly, and see it visibly—for, if London is the right hand of the world—its active, mighty right hand—then we may regard that street which leads from the Exchange to Downing Street as the world's radial artery.

But send no poet to London! This downright earnestness of all things, this colossal uniformity, this machine-like movement, this moroseness even in pleasure, this exaggerated London, smothers the imagination and rends the heart. And should you ever send a German poet thither—a dreamer, who stands staring at every single phenomenon, even a ragged beggar-woman, or a shining jeweller's shop— why, then he will find things going badly with him, and he will be hustled about on every side, or even be knocked over with a mild "God damn!" God damn!—the damned pushing!

I soon saw that these people have much to do. They live on a large scale, and though food and clothes are dearer with them than with us, they must still be better fed and clothed than we are—as gentility requires. Moreover, they have enormous debts, yet occasionally in a vainglorious mood they make ducks and drakes of their guineas, pay other nations to fight for their pleasure, give their respective kings a handsome *douceur* into the bargain—and, therefore, John Bull must work day and night to get the money for such expenses; by day and by night he must tax his brain to discover new machines, and he sits and reckons in the sweat of his brow, and runs and rushes without looking about much from the docks to the Exchange, and from the Exchange to the Strand, and, therefore, it is quite pardonable if, when a poor German poet, gazing into a print-shop window, stands in his way at the corner of Cheapside, he should knock him aside with a rather rough "God damn!"

Heinrich Heine

At Bossekop

LATER IN the day, while ski-ing on the slopes above the village, I heard the distant tinkling of bells, and soon, over the brow of the hill, I saw the arrival of a long caravan of laden sledges. They were in single file, each drawn by a reindeer, which was fastened by a leather thong to the back of the sledge in front. The caravan was divided into many " strings ", the latter consisting of ten to twelve sledges and reindeer linked together as described, and each string being in charge of a Lapp driver whose business it was to keep the traces disentangled, and at sharp corners or when going downhill to see that the sledges did not overturn. The Lapp is very skilful in his management of the reindeer on a cross-country journey. He is helped by his dogs, which often lead the caravan and find the winter tracks, cheering on the reindeer when they begin to tire by running backwards and forwards in front, and barking as if to encourage them, or snapping at their legs should they prove lazy.

The reindeer is the Laplander's most valued possession, and his main support, providing him with food, milk and clothing, and being the sole means of transport through the winter snows both for himself and his goods. . . .

A Lapp's wealth depends on the number of deer he owns, for the people do not count their riches in terms of money, but by the number of reindeer in their possession. A rich Lapp will often own a thousand deer or more, and his necessities, mainly coffee, salt and snuff or tobacco, are so few that he will often increase the number of his herd by the money he makes trading in reindeer meat and furs, or by the tools carved from the animal's bones. Every part of the reindeer is utilized in some form or other, even the sinews and hair, the former being sold to merchants who export them for thread in surgery, and the latter being disposed of in large quantities for the stuffing of life-belts, for each hair of a reindeer is a hollow tube, filled with air and unsinkable.

Reindeer are wonderful swimmers and, when the great spring migration to the coast takes place, thousands may be seen swimming the fjords, which they must cross before they can reach one of the islands near Hammerfest, where many of them spend the summer months. The Lapps are forced to follow where the reindeer lead, it is impossible for them to keep back the herd when it decides to move; their movements are thus ruled by their deer. The animals do not all migrate to the coast, many of those in Swedish Lapland merely cross the border into Norway, spending the summer up in the high fells of Finmark, while others move towards Tromsö. The calving time is in May, when the herd is generally moving to its summer quarters. Many of the mothers have a special preference for certain valleys, and nothing will induce them to leave till after the birth of their calves.

Olive Murray Chapman

The African Nubas

THE NUBAS of Solara, the village where we are to camp, have heard of our coming, and are swarming down the valley to meet us. Some have stopped by mud pools and are doing their toilets. There could be no greater mistake than to suppose that because they have no clothes they dispense with this part of the human routine. Far from it. Their hair is done in elaborate patterns picked out with safety-pins. Their bodies are washed and polished, oil rubbed in till they glisten like mahogany. Many of them are adorning themselves for the occasion with pale grey mud picked from the pools and worked into original designs on their black bodies. Some of these designs are obviously caricatures of clothes. One has got himself up like an Arab office-boy he has seen at Dilling, with short-sleeved tunic reaching to the knees rubbed in with mud, and black skin left about the waist to show where the boy wears a sash. Very effective. Another is similarly adorned with a mud jumper and shorts.

Nearly all wear necklaces, bangles, nose-rings or ear-rings, and the women have bead belts of various colours showing whether they are single, married or affianced. Newly initiated young men wear fur collars, and women who have recently had babies long strips of fur down their backs. As we come up to the village five or six hundred are gathered on the flat space in front of the rest-house in readiness for the dance which is to celebrate our visit. The women break into the *ulalele*—the shrill, burbling chorus which is the sign of welcome—and the elders advance offering both hands.

Follows a long pause in which certain young men prance about with enormous swagger, but nothing else happens. Then it is conveyed to us that something has gone wrong. The drum is broken and they cannot dance without it. We produce a tray and a stick to beat it with, but the idea is either not understood or summarily rejected. It takes half an hour to get another drum, and the time is filled with more prancings by the young men and incessant clapping of hands. At last the new drum arrives, and to its beating the whole crowd gets in motion. They go slowly round a circle in single file, young men, old men, girls, brides, married women, each in a separate formation, never touching or mingling with the others, but just walking round and round and stamping their feet. The children seem to go as they please, running about and dodging between the groups. A few of the men have spears which they brandish, but most are content with the strong straight poles which nearly everybody in this country seems to carry. They shout and laugh as they go round, and the general effect is that of a glistening mass of black humanity revolving in the sun.

There is a curious lack of finish about it all. You always think that something more is going to happen, but nothing more ever does happen.

J. A. Spender

Old Man of the Sea

IN THE evening we came back restlessly to the top of the deck-house, and we discussed the Old Man of the Sea, who might well be a myth, except that too many people have seen him. There is some quality in man which makes him people the ocean with monsters and one wonders whether they are there or not. In one sense they are, for we continue to see them. One afternoon in the laboratory ashore we sat drinking coffee and talking with Jimmy Costello, who is a reporter on the Monterey *Herald*. The telephone rang and his city editor said that the decomposed body of a sea-serpent was washed up on the beach at Moss Landing, half-way around the Bay. Jimmy was to rush over and get pictures of it. He rushed, approached the evil-smelling monster from which the flesh was dropping. There was a note pinned to its head which said, " Don't worry about it, it's a basking shark. (Signed) Dr. Rolph Bolin of the Hopkins Marine Station." No doubt that Dr. Bolin acted kindly, for he loves true things; but his kindness was a blow to the people of Monterey. They so wanted it to be a sea-serpent. Even we hoped it would be.

When sometime a true sea-serpent, completed and undecayed, is found or caught, a shout of triumph will go through the world. " There, you see," men will say, " I knew they were there all the time. I just had a feeling they were there." Men really need sea-monsters in their personal oceans. And the Old Man of the Sea is one of these. In Monterey you can find many people who have seen him. Tiny Colletto has seen him close up and can draw a crabbed sketch of him. He is very large. He stands up in the water, three or four feet emerged above the waves, and watches an approaching boat until it comes too close, and then he sinks slowly out of sight. He looks somewhat like a tremendous diver, with large eyes and fur shaggily hanging from him.

So far, he has not been photographed. When he is, probably Dr. Bolin will identify him and another beautiful story will be shattered. For this reason we rather hope he is never photographed, for if the Old Man of the Sea should turn out to be some great malformed sea-lion, a lot of people would feel a sharp personal loss—a Santa Claus loss. And the ocean would be none the better for it. For the ocean, deep and black in the depths, is like the low dark levels of our minds in which the dream symbols incubate and sometimes rise up to sight like the Old Man of the Sea.

John Steinbeck and Edward F. Ricketts

The Rickshaw

THE REV. J. FORDYCE, a Chaplain of St. Mark's Church, was much troubled by the uncomfortable thoughts of death and dignity which arose in the minds of his congregation in the Victorian age. And, being very concerned to see that the souls of his flock did not suffer from the discomforts of the body, he concentrated all his efforts to secure an adequate vehicle for the conveyance of their persons from their bungalows to the Church and from the Church to their bungalows. He invented the rickshaw. The people of Simla still remember his magnificent model:

The hood of that first rickshaw
Was square and trimmed with fringe,
Such as dangled from the mantelpiece,
In many a Berlin tinge.

During the early eighties
When Reverend Fordyce J.
Invented the first rickshaw
For Simla during May.

It was not difficult to train coolies to run like horses. So that soon the jampans and dandis had been ousted and the rickshaw came in. And, of course, the genius of western man for technical achievement improved vastly on the original model in the decades following the death of Reverend J. Fordyce. The first rickshaw was iron-tyred and, it is said, used to bump and shake fearfully. On the night of a big dance or other *tamasha*, Simla used to be kept up by the continual rumbling roll of hundreds of rickshaws. The rubber tyre was introduced in 1898, and in 1904 the Municipality made it a condition for securing a licence that a rickshaw should have rubber tyres, in view of the constant wear and tear of the road by the iron wheels. Pneumatic tyres came next. With this, and improvements in cushions and upholstery, it is now a pleasure for the rich to be driven about in rickshaws, especially as they do not disturb slumbering Simla on their return from all-night revelries. Old Gandhi refused to ride in a rickshaw as, he said, it hurt his soul to have to be borne in a carriage driven by human beings. Local opinion concurred that he was the greatest crank in history.

The usual length of the Simla rickshaw is nine feet, including the shaft, and the breadth is four feet. The weight is normally 260 to 360 lb., exclusive of the weight of the ladies and gentlemen who ride in them. The coolies curse the weight of the rickshaw in their hearts sometimes when they are driving uphill, and swear under their breath against the balance when occupied by too opulent a majesty: things, however, which the passengers never notice as they lean back while the men heave and push it from the back bar strenuously.

Mulk Raj Anand

The Natives of New Holland

FROM WHAT I have said of the Natives of New Holland they may appear to some to be the most wretched People upon Earth; but in reality they are far more happier than we Europeans, being wholly unacquainted not only with the Superfluous, but with the necessary Conveniences so much sought after in Europe; they are happy in not knowing the use of them. They live in a Tranquility which is not disturbed by the Inequality of Condition. The Earth and Sea of their own accord furnishes them with all things necessary for Life.

They covet not Magnificent Houses, Household-stuff, etc.; they live in a Warm and fine Climate, and enjoy every wholesome Air, so that they have very little need of Cloathing; and this they seem to be fully sensible of, for many to whom we gave Cloth, etc., left it carelessly upon the Sea beach and in the Woods, as a thing they had no manner of use for; in short, they seem'd to set no Value upon anything we gave them, nor would they ever part with anything of their own for any one Article we could offer them. This, in my opinion, Argues that they think themselves provided with all the necessarys of Life, and that they have no Superfluities.

Captain James Cook

An American Abroad

I WAS ALWAYS fond of visiting new scenes, and observing strange characters and manners. Even when a mere child I began my travels, and made many tours of discovery into foreign parts and unknown regions of my native city, to the frequent alarm of my parents, and the emolument of the town-crier. As I grew into boyhood, I extended the range of my observations. My holiday afternoons were spent in rambles about the surrounding country. I made myself familiar with all its places famous in history or fable. I knew every spot where a murder or robbery had been committed, or a ghost seen. I visited the neighbouring villages, and added greatly to my stock of knowledge by noting their habits and customs, and conversing with their sages and great men. I even journeyed one long summer's day to the summit of the most distant hill, whence I stretched my eye over many a mile of *terra incognita*, and was astonished to find how vast a globe I inhabited.

This rambling propensity strengthened with my years. Books of voyages and travels became my passion, and in devouring their contents I neglected the regular exercises of the school. How wistfully would I wander about the pierheads in fine weather, and watch the parting ships bound to distant climes—with what longing eyes would I gaze after their lessening sails, and waft myself in imagination to the ends of the earth!

Further reading and thinking, though they brought this vague inclination into more reasonable bounds, only served to make it more decided. I visited various parts of my own country; and had I been merely a lover of fine scenery, I should have felt little desire to seek elsewhere its gratification; for on no country have the charms of Nature been more prodigally lavished. Her mighty lakes, like oceans of liquid silver; her mountains, with their bright aerial tints; her valleys, teeming with wild fertility; her tremendous cataracts, thundering in their solitudes; her boundless plains, waving with spontaneous verdure; her broad deep rivers, rolling in solemn silence to the ocean; her trackless forests, where vegetation puts forth all its magnificence; her skies, kindling with the magic of summer clouds and glorious sunshine;—no, never need an American look beyond his own country for the sublime and beautiful of natural scenery.

But Europe held forth the charms of storied and poetical association. There were to be seen the masterpieces of art, the refinements of highly cultivated society, the quaint peculiarities of ancient and local custom. My native country was full of youthful promise: Europe was rich in the accumulated treasures of age. Her very ruins told the history of times gone by, and every mouldering stone was a chronicle. I longed to wander over the scenes of renowned achievement—to tread, as it were, in the footsteps of antiquity—to loiter about the ruined castle— to meditate on the falling tower—to escape, in short, from the commonplace realities of the present, and lose myself among the shadowy grandeurs of the past.

I had, beside all this, an earnest desire to see the great men of the earth. We have, it is true, our great men in America; not a city but has an ample share of them. I have mingled among them in my time, and been almost withered by the shade into which they cast me; for there is nothing so baneful to a small man as the shade of a great one, particularly the great man of the city. But I was anxious to see the great men of Europe; for I had read in the works of various philosophers, that all animals degenerated in America, and man among the number. A great man of Europe, thought I, must therefore be as superior to a great man of America as a peak of the Alps to a highland of the Hudson; and in this idea I was confirmed, by observing the comparative importance and swelling magnitude of many English travellers among us, who, I was assured, were very little people in their own country. I will visit this land of wonders, thought I, and see the gigantic race from which I am degenerated.

It has been either my good or evil lot to have my roving passion gratified. I have wandered through different countries, and witnessed many of the shifting scenes of life. I cannot say that I have studied them with the eyes of a philosopher; but rather with the sauntering gaze with which humble lovers of the picturesque stroll from the window of one print-shop to another; caught sometimes by the delineations of beauty, sometimes by the distortions of caricature, and sometimes by the loveliness of landscape. As it is the fashion for modern tourists to travel pencil in hand, and bring home their portfolios filled with sketches, I am disposed to get up a few for the entertainment of my friends. When, however, I look over the hints and memorandums I have taken down for the purpose, my heart almost fails me at finding how my idle humour has led me aside from the great objects studied by every regular traveller who would make a book. I fear I shall give equal disappointment with an unlucky landscape painter who had travelled on the Continent, but, following the bent of his vagrant inclination, had sketched in nooks, and corners, and by-places. His sketch-book was accordingly crowded with cottages, and landscapes, and obscure ruins; for he had neglected to paint St. Peter's or the Coliseum, the cascade of Terni or the bay of Naples, and had not a single glacier or volcano in his whole collection.

Washington Irving

Marco Polo at the Court of Kubla Khan

IT IS WELL ascertained that the Tartars date the commencement of their year from the month of February, and on that occasion it is customary for the grand khan, as well as all who are subject to him, in their several countries, to clothe themselves in white garments, which, according to their ideas, are the emblems of good fortune; and they assume this dress at the beginning of the year, in the hope that, during the whole course of it, nothing but what is fortunate may happen to them, and that they may enjoy pleasure and comfort. Upon this day the inhabitants of all the provinces and kingdoms who hold lands or rights of jurisdiction under the grand khan, send him valuable presents of gold, silver, and precious stones, together with many pieces of white cloth, which they add, with the intent that His Majesty may experience throughout the year uninterrupted felicity, and possess treasures adequate to all his expenses. . . .

On the morning of the festival, before the tables are spread, all the princes, the nobility of various ranks, the cavaliers, astrologers, physicians, and falconers, with many others holding public offices, the prefects of the people and of the lands, together with the officers of the army, make their entry into the grand hall, in front of the emperor. Those who cannot find room within, stand on the outside of the building, in such a situation as to be within sight of their sovereign. The assemblage is marshalled in the following order. The first places are assigned to the sons and grandsons of his majesty and all the imperial family. Next to these are the provincial kings and the nobility of the empire, according to their several degrees, in regular succession.

When all have been disposed in the places appointed for them, a person of high dignity, or as we should express it, a great prelate, rises and says with a loud voice: " Bow down and do reverence "; when instantly all bend their bodies until their foreheads touch the floor. Again the prelate cries: " God bless our lord, and long preserve him in the enjoyment of felicity." To which the people answer: " God grant it." Once more the prelate says: " May God increase the grandeur and prosperity of his empire; may he preserve all those who are his subjects in the blessings of peace and contentment; and in all their lands may abundance prevail." The people again reply: " God grant it." They then make prostrations four times.

This being done, the prelate advances to an altar, richly adorned, upon which is placed a red tablet inscribed with the name of the grand khan. Near to this stands a censer of burning incense, with which the prelate, on the behalf of all who are assembled, perfumes the tablet and the altar, in a reverential manner; when every one present humbly prostrates himself before the tablet. This ceremony being concluded, they return to their places, and then make the presentation of their respective gifts; such as have been mentioned. When a display has been made of these, and the grand khan has cast his eyes upon them, the tables are prepared for the feast, and the company, as well women as men, arrange themselves there in the manner and order described in a former chapter. Upon the removal of the victuals, the musicians and theatrical performers exhibit for the amusement of the court, as has already been related. But on this occasion a lion is conducted into the presence of his majesty, so tame, that it is taught to lay itself down at his feet. The sports being finished, every one returns to his own home.

Marco Polo

Easter in Jerusalem

THE NEXT day, the Latin Easter, and the Orthodox Palm Sunday, the confusion and the crowd were even more remarkable. At the Austrian (Latin) Hospice where we lodged the feast began with a breakfast of hard-boiled and brightly coloured eggs and some sweet and sticky bread, somewhat trying to the untrained stomach. More eggs, gold and silver and striped and mottled, and more sweet bread were piled in the stalls along the streets, as we pressed with the throng of pilgrims towards the Sepulchre.

The square before the Church was so packed that only the unrelenting elbows of our dragoman enabled us to pass, or, once inside the building, to reach the chancel where the Greek service was being held, and at last to attain a position of comparative safety upon the chancel steps. Below, the pushing and movement was incessant—although the crowd looked so thick that you would have thought it impossible to move. But the Latins were holding their Easter Mass in the Franciscan Chapel, and all the Orthodox were determined to reach the chancel, or at least, from the body of the rotunda, to see something of the splendid Greek ritual.

Splendid to the eye it certainly was. The Greek Patriarch, set round with a great throng of priests and monks (they come in from all the convents of the neighbourhood), was robed in vestments of pale gold and white, exquisitely worked, and from this shimmering radiance their dark faces gleamed out with theatrical effectiveness. Each held in his hand a little Victorian posy of bright flowers—a remnant, doubtless, of the days when herbs were carried as a protection against the plague. (I myself should have been glad of a scented posy, and this also for practical reasons.)

The congregation held—and waved—palms and lighted candles, both a source of pain and danger to their neighbours. The chanting was monotonous and soothing, but the service seemed interminable—the changing of places, the changing of vestments, the Gospel reading, and then, again, the low and droning chants. And, pressed as we were against the hot Greek pilgrims, I began to fear that I should not be able to endure until the end. As I looked round for a way of escape there came a stir, a movement, even a blessed breath of air—the Procession was forming. It seemed impossible that it should pass through the dense mass of people, but the relentless banging of the ushers' staves, so close to unprotected feet, induced compression, and the long train of priests and monks and acolytes passed down the steps, and then, at last, the ivory-faced old Patriarch himself, under the silken canopy.

As we slipped out, behind the procession, into the cool emptiness of the Chapel of the Invention of the Cross, before attempting to make our way to the only door which led to the open air, we thought of the horror of a fire in such a place, where long veils and waving palms and candles are in close proximity, and there is only one small aperture for escape. But as every stone of the church is sacred and the property of some communion, it is said to be impossible to make even a small emergency door. The priests of every creed, it seemed, preferred to run the risk of death at every feast, rather than relinquish a fragment of their holy heritage.

Lady Sybil Lubbock

Within the Orchid Door

AFTER LUNCH in Shun-ko's room, served to us by Sweet Rain and Bald-the-third, a serving matron came from Kuei-tzu, wife of the Family Elder and Lady of First Authority, to say that if I was now rested the Orchid Door would receive me. Shun-ko explained that this was a command for me to now make a formal call in each house in the woman's part of the homestead.

She rehearsed me in a bow " sapling swept by the wind ", told me I must always accept a tea-cup into the palms of both hands, and to walk backwards slowly and gracefully when taking leave.

We went first to the Garden of Children. The nice little boys and girls in residence there were solemnly ceremonious. When we had exchanged bows, the elder of the girls poured tea into rose-patterned cups and the two eldest boys passed it with sugared dates. The Spring-time Bower, to which girls graduate from the Garden of Children, came next. Mai-da received me formally in the house I shared with her but then accompanied us to the house of the twins, Ching-mei and La-mei, and the houses of Shou-su and Li-niang.

This afternoon, and for many following weeks, I felt myself in a maze of courts and a maze of persons—all alike and yet each different. There were then thirty-six women mated to Lins. Each woman in the House of Exile has her own house furnished and decorated according to her taste and dowry. Shun-ko was careful to have me stay just as long in the homes of women who wear the green skirt as in the homes of wives: in the House of Exile, Li-la, the first mother, wore the green skirt. Through these calls (excepting the one to Sung-li, who hated and feared all foreigners because at seven years of age she had seen a foreign soldier rape her mother in the days of terror following on the siege of Peking in 1900, and had protested in Family Council against my coming) my hostesses whether of serious or gay temperament all made me feel that they were glad I had come. I felt elated.

The sun was singing an evening anthem in the sky above the courts as I went to audience with Kuei-tzu, Lady of First Authority. I made my bow. I accepted my cup of tea carefully in the palms of both hands. She addressed me. Shun-ko translated her speech into English. I replied in English.

Before Shun-ko could translate, Kuei-tzu made a sound like ice tinkling in a glass. Shun-ko whispered to me to bend my head near to the floor and go away. I did.

Shun-ko followed me into the court. She told me that Kuei-tzu had said that I was to be taken from her sight and not to be shown to her again until I was sufficiently civilized to hear and to speak, and given the command that no member of the Family was ever again to communicate with me in any language except Chinese.

It had been arranged that my arrival would be announced to the ancestors on the evening of the same day as my introduction to the women and children. The First Lady's dismissal of me postponed this ceremony for a considerable time. Eventually, however, my ear, my brain, and my tongue were a three-stringed guitar on which I could play sufficiently well to be presented for examination. After a half-hour oral examination, the Lady in First Authority pronounced me civilized.

Then the Hall of Ancestors was swept again. Laurel incense was bought. The family gathered within the circle of generations. The Elder told the ancestors about me. As previously instructed, I lit a candle before each tablet of which there is one for each man and woman whose earthly life is woven into the homestead past.

The morning after this ceremony, I was told that I was " daughter-by-affection ", now and forever, not just to Shun-ko my sponsor, but to the entire clan of Lin.

Nora Waln

Life in Addis Ababa

EVERY DAY is market day in Addis Ababa. The crowd is partly composed of the people of the town, and partly of the inhabitants of the surrounding villages. It is in a perpetual clamour from morning to night, like a huge uproarious hive of bees. The air is laden with loathsome dust, and the mixed smell of vegetables, perspiring Africans, spices, and scents is indescribable.

Sometimes the mob is broken for a moment to permit the passage of a European man and woman riding in to make purchases or to pay calls. There is little in the market which is calculated to appeal to European tastes, and in almost everything their wants are supplied directly from Europe. The Abyssinians from the distant villages will stop and gape at these white people, the like of whom they may have never seen in the course of their lives, but the remainder of the crowd, more accustomed to such sights, will quickly push and jostle the peasants and send them reeling into circulation again.

Then a chief comes by, riding a diminutive horse or mule. He is surrounded by a bare-foot nondescript escort of men-at-arms, carrying rifles. They hop along with their chief, seeming to imitate the jerky gait of his horse, whose paces are entirely untrained. The chief wears a short black cloak of a European fashion, a mark of his superior station. Two brass studs and a small chain invariably adorn the collar of the cloak. In some cases the garment is of blue velvet. The head of such a personage is crowned with a big grey hat, and altogether he contrasts oddly with the general crowd; their uncovered woolly heads, their flowing shroud-like *chammas*. The members of the escort contend for a place near their master. It is enough to succeed in placing a hand on the withers of his horse, or on the saddle, stirrups, bridle—anywhere so long as direct contact is made with the animal he rides and so with the chief himself. Thus encircled about, almost as though borne along by the perspiring retinue, the grey hat and the great man under it move along. And then, since it is above all things necessary to impart to the world the impression that he is concerned with affairs of great import, the chief and his jostling escort move with preoccupied dispatch. So, trotting and hopping hurriedly, the group proceeds on its way, nor, if there are people abroad to watch it, does it abate its rapid pace even when going uphill. The climb will end somewhere; an easier road will follow, a road empty of men, and then the panting men-at-arms will be free to pause and walk more slowly and recover their breath, as does a village brass band on the day of its patron saint.

Sometimes two of these hurrying clusters of humanity will come face to face. For a moment their progress is checked; they hesitate, each party backs a little and its members crowd together. Keen glances are directed by each at the other. Each is summing-up the "importance" of the other and contrasting it with its own. In a few moments it becomes clear as to which side must give way, but this is done with dignity, with no diminution of self-esteem. All Abyssinians are inordinately proud.

L. M. Nesbitt

Making an African King

DURING THE days of mourning the old men of the village busied themselves in choosing a new king. This also is a secret operation. The choice is made in private, and communicated to the populace only on the seventh day, when the new king is to be crowned. But the king is kept ignorant of his good fortune to the last.

It happened that Njogoni, a good friend of my own, was elected. The choice fell on him, in part because he came of a good family, but chiefly because he was a favourite of the people and could get the most votes. I do not know that Njogoni had the slightest suspicion of his elevation. At any rate, if he had, he shammed ignorance very well. As he was walking on the shore, on the morning of the seventh day, he was suddenly set upon by the entire populace, who proceeded to a ceremony which is preliminary to the crowning, and which must deter any but the most ambitious men from aspiring to the crown. They surrounded him in a dense crowd, and then began to heap upon him every manner of abuse that the worst of mobs could imagine. Some spit in his face; some beat him with their fists; some kicked him; others threw disgusting objects at him; while those unlucky ones who stood on the outside, and could reach the poor fellow only with their voices, assiduously cursed him, his father, his mother, his sisters and brothers, and all his ancestors to the remotest generation. A stranger would not have given a cent for the life of him who was presently to be crowned.

Amid all the noise and struggle, I caught the words which explained all this to me; for every few minutes some fellow, administering an especially severe blow or kick, would shout out, "You are not our king yet; for a little while we will do what we please with you. By-and-by we shall have to do your will."

Njogoni bore himself like a man and a prospective king. He kept his temper, and took all the abuse with a smiling face. When it had lasted about half an hour, they took him to the house of the old king. Here he was seated, and became again for a little while the victim of his people's curses.

Then all became silent; and the elders of the people rose and said, solemnly (the people repeating after them), "Now we choose you for our king: we engage to listen to you and to obey you."

A silence followed, and presently the silk hat, which is the emblem of Mpongwe royalty, was brought in and placed on Njogoni's head. He was then dressed in a red gown, and received the greatest marks of respect from all who had just now abused him.

Paul B. du Chaillu

The Totem

AT ONE time the Bamangwato venerated the crocodile, which seems to have been the original totem of all the branches of the Bechuana peoples. The change is said to have come about in the following way. Long ago the Bamangwato were engaged in war and their chief, being driven by his enemies, fled. They followed hard on his heels and, as it was very hot, he almost fainted on the way. At last he saw in the near distance a thicket and to it he ran and hid himself therein, thinking that his enemies, who, he thought, had not seen him enter the thicket, would pass by, believing that he was still on ahead. Some were of the opinion that he was in the thicket, and when they drew near they shouted at the top of their voices, saying they had caught him. But a duiker [a small antelope], alarmed by the shouting, leaped from the thicket as they approached it. Seeing the duiker rush from the bush they concluded that no man had gone into it, otherwise it would not have remained there till they came up. So they passed on.

After they had gone the chief came from his hiding-place, and as his life had been saved by the duiker he gave orders that from that day the duiker should be the totem of his tribe. So today the Bamangwato venerate the duiker. Not only is it not killed, but its skin is not used by the people for any purpose whatever. Its flesh is not eaten, and so great was the veneration or fear in which the father of the late chief of the Bamangwato held the duiker that on seeing a duiker mat at the door of the house of a European he was visiting it had to be removed before he would enter the house. And although today the taboo has lost its significance for many members of this tribe, I do not think any would be found who would eat the flesh or use the skin of the duiker.

J. Tom Brown

Gipsies

THE SNOW falls deep; the forest lies alone;
The boy goes hasty for his load of brakes,
Then thinks upon the fire and hurries back;
The gipsy knocks his hands and tucks them up,
And seeks his squalid camp, half hid in snow,
Beneath the oak which breaks away the wind,
And bushes close in snow-like hovel warm;
There tainted mutton wastes upon the coals,
And the half-wasted dog squats close and rubs,
Then feels the heat too strong, and goes aloof;
He watches well, but none a bit can spare,
And vainly waits the morsel thrown away.
'Tis thus they live—a picture to the place,
A quiet, pilfering, unprotected race.

John Clare

An Eastern Magician

I FOUND there my friend, John Henry Middleton, the old Cambridge professor, an old ally of Morris's and intimate in former days with Rossetti. Middleton had been a considerable traveller in out-of-the-way places, and he narrated to me in detail what I had already heard him tell, his experience in Morocco with a Moorish magician.

He was travelling in 1879 about half-way between Tetuan and Morocco, and one evening an old man came to his camp mounted on an ass, with a boy as servant. The man said he was a magician, and proposed to perform three wonders; the first to throw a ball of twine into the air, the second to make a plant grow, and the third to show the face of a person thought of, in a globe of ink. It was already late, and the performance was put off until the following morning—the magician remaining the night in the camp, and in the morning when the tents were struck he was invited to give his performance. It was an open place, uninhabited, and without trees or bushes. Middleton chose the ground at some little distance from where the camp had been. The magician first took from his wallet a large ball of string, large enough to need both hands to lift it, and, having made a long incantation, he tied the end of the string to one finger of his left hand, and then with great exertion threw the ball upwards, which unravelled as it went, and, growing less and less, disappeared in the air. He then let go of the string's end, which continued to hang from the sky. The magician and his boy sat at a little distance, and Middleton went to the string and pulled it downwards, as you would pull a bell-rope. It stretched to within about two feet of the ground, but he felt the resistance strongly from above, so much so that he cut his fingers with the string, the mark remaining for several days afterwards. The five men whom he had with him also touched the string, three of those were Moors, one a Berber, and the other an interpreter. It was clear daylight at the time, about half an hour after sunrise. When they had all satisfied themselves that the string was suspended as it appeared to be, the magician came forward, and in his turn pulled it, when it fell down from the sky in coils on the ground; he then rolled it up again into a ball, and put it back into his wallet.

The magician next took from his wallet a seed, and, when Middleton had chosen a bare place, planted it in the ground; he then asked for some palm branches which they had with them, and which had been cut the day before, and he made an arched covering with them over the seed and heaped horse rugs upon the hoops, and then sat apart and made incantations.

At the end of a few minutes he invited them to undo the covering, and there, in the ground, a plant was growing, set firmly in the earth, the first time a few inches high, but when he had covered it up again and built the hoops higher, it at last became three feet eight inches high. Middleton measured the plant, found it firmly rooted, and cut off and kept some of the leaves; the nature of the plant seemed to resemble that of the India-rubber tree, and it had some fifty leaves. It was fresh and healthy though the weather was very hot, it being the month of October. In the third incantation Middleton was made to look into a globe of ink. He desired to see the face of a friend, but instead saw persistently and very vividly a certain landscape he knew well on the River Severn, near Tewkesbury. The magician when asked whether he could climb the string and disappear in the air (like the magician Marco Polo tells of) stated that his grandfather had the power, but that he himself was unable. Having been rewarded, he mounted his ass and rode away. Middleton believes that the manifestations produced were mesmeric, certainly no trick. The leaves of the plant he kept for some time, but lost with other things in a shipwreck on his way home.

Wilfrid Scawen Blunt

To Exiles

ARE YOU not weary in your distant places,
    Far, far from Scotland of the mist and storm,
In drowsy airs, the sun-smite on your faces,
    The days so long and warm?
When all around you lie the strange fields sleeping,
    The dreary woods where no fond memories roam,
Do not your sad hearts over seas come leaping
    To the highlands and the lowlands of your Home?

Wild cries the Winter, loud through all our valleys
    The midnights roar, the grey noons echo back;
About the scalloped coasts the eager galleys
    Beat for kind harbours from horizons black;
We tread the miry roads, the rain-drenched heather,
    We are the men, we battle, we endure!
God's pity for you people in your weather
    Of swooning winds, calm seas, and skies demure!

Wild cries the Winter, and we walk song-haunted
    Over the hills and by the thundering falls,
Or where the dirge of a brave past is chaunted ·
    In dolorous dusks by immemorial walls.
Though rains may beat us and the great mists blind us,
    And lightning rend the pine-tree on the hill,
Yet are we strong, yet shall the morning find us
    Children of tempest all unshaken still.

We wander where the little grey towns cluster
    Deep in the hills, or selvedging the sea,
By farm-lands lone, by woods where wildfowl muster

To shelter from the day's inclemency;
And night will come, and then far through the darkling,
 A light will shine out in the sounding glen,
And it will mind us of some fond eye's sparkling,
 And we'll be happy then.

Let torrents pour then, let the great winds rally,
 Snow-silence fall or lightning blast the pine;
That light of Home shines warmly in the valley,
 And, exiled son of Scotland, it is thine.
Far have you wandered over seas of longing,
 And now you drowse, and now you well may weep,
When all the recollections come a-thronging
 Of this old country where your fathers sleep.

They sleep, but still the hearth is warmly glowing
 While the wild Winter blusters round their land;
That light of Home, the wind so bitter blowing—
 Look, look and listen, do you understand?
Love, strength, and tempest—oh, come back and share them!
 Here is the cottage, here the open door;
Fond are our hearts although we do not bare them,—
 They're yours, and you are ours for evermore.

Neil Munro

In Passing

FOREIGN TRAVEL oftentimes makes many to wander from themselves
as well as from their country, and to come back mere mimics; and so
in going far to fare worse, and bring back less wit than they carried
forth. They go out figures (according to the Italian proverb) and
return ciphers. They retain the vice of a country, and will discourse
learnedly thereon, but pass by and forget the good, their memories
being herein like hair-sieves, that keep up the bran and let go the
fine flour. They strive to degenerate as much as they can from
Englishmen, and all their talk is still foreign, or at least will bring it
to be so, though it be by head and shoulders, magnifying other
nations, and derogating from their own. Nor can one hardly exchange
three words with them at an ordinary (or elsewhere) but presently they

are th'other side of the sea, commending either the wines of France, the fruits of Italy, or the oil and salads of Spain.

Some also there are who by their countenance more than by their carriage, by their diseases more than by their discourses, discover themselves to have been abroad under hot climates.

Others have a custom to be always relating strange things and wonders (of the humour of Sir John Mandeville), and they usually present them to the hearers through multiplying glasses, and thereby cause the thing to appear far greater than it is in itself. They make mountains out of mole-hills, like Charenton bridge echo, which doubles the sound nine times. Such a traveller was he, that reported the Indian fly to be as big as a fox, China birds to be as big as some horses, and their mice to be as big as monkeys. But they have the wit to fetch this far enough off, because the hearer may rather believe it than make a voyage so far to disprove it.

James Howell

PLACES

Place Names

AND WHAT lovely sounds they are; what images they summon up . . . Piacenza . . . Cremona . . . Guastalla . . . Mirandola . . . Carpi . . . Concordia . . . Gonzaga . . . Crevalcore. . . .

First there is Piacenza, the City of Pleasance, the happiest name, as it may be, in all the world; a flower-scented city of dark blues and greens, dark rusty cypresses against a luminous evening sky; of peacocks spreading their tails and drumming out their feathers on a lawn, of cool, green tunnels, fountains, and cascades under the shelter of blue, sloping hills, and pastures for antelope and gazelle: and far away, hidden under its sound, the illicit, because too concrete, materialization of a Gothic castle, built of the most inappropriate green marble; a Byronic fantasy anchored to reality among the vales and crags of Greece, still littered with the fragments of the antique world, by that Duchess of Pleasance who was the widow of one of Napoleon's generals. Next comes Cremona, a bone-thin, lemon-coloured city of music, assuming in the mind the shape of a three-arched bridge, of which the middle syllable forms the chief span: then follow Guastalla, like Gonzaga, the proudest of sumptuous Spanish names, cities of tents, pitched, it seems, for conquering grandees, of black and sepia velvet heavily encrusted with gold; Mirandola, most perfectly balanced of musical sounds, associated for ever with poetry, a town of the early Renaissance waiting in an enchanted captivity for the first tourist to release it; Carpi, an ancient, silver-scaled city, ever grumbling to itself in its golden plain of times past and gone by; Concordia, formal, classic city of repose, with wide vistas composed of palaces and churches, with statues on tall pillars and a certain peaceful deadness in its broad and empty streets; Crevalcore, gay, Polish citadel of the waltz and the mazurka, placed incongruously among murmuring streams and mulberry-trees: so to me they appear, abstract and unattainable, shaped out of nothingness by the outline, rhythm, and intonation of their syllables. . . . How lovely they are in their music, how individual and full of personality, never falling into couples, inseparable as Castor and Pollux, Romulus and Remus, as do the towns of the Campania and Two Sicilies, where we find Caltagirone and Caltanisetta, Galatone and Galatina (those twin names, succulent and truffled, spiritual birth-

place, surely, of all Italian cooks and warehousemen), and the two
tumbling clowns of the Adriatic, Bitonto and Bitetto, sad and decaying
Romanesque cities, yet bearing names that would ensure the fortune
of any comic turn on the English music-hall stage.

Yes . . . Mirandola . . . Carpi . . . Guastalla . . . Crevalcore
. . . Piacenza . . . Gonzaga . . . Cremona . . . Concordia. These
are the most beautifully named cities in Italy, perhaps in the world.
. . . They lack, you may protest, the sound of the obsidian battle-axe
that still lives in the place-names of Mexico; Tehuentepec or Oaxaca;
the savage gong and tom-tom symphony that issues from many African
cities, Timgad, Kairouan, Marrakeesh, and Mogador—especially from
Mogador, crenellated fortress of sullen and endless yellow tides, that
in the exclamatory horror of its syllables still retains the lingering terror
of the slave-trade, when slaves white and black, chained together,
dragging under the whip through the sultry heats of cruel and ashen
deserts, were driven thither, to be embarked like cattle; the uncouth,
tropical clumsiness exhaled by the sound of others—Timbuctoo,
Tozeur, and Figuig, sounds as strange and evil-smelling as tropical
fruit, names of morose metropolises hidden among mangrove swamps
or concealed in the ambushes set by sand for the wind, places

> Where Sirocco and Simoom
> Battle with hot breath for room.

They are wanting, it may be, in the drowsy, sonorous, fat comfort of
East Anglian village names, Boreham, and Great Snoring (and, for
that matter, Little Snoring, too); in the inflated self-importance of
Bombay, capital of Babu bombast which lies sweltering under its
crimson skies; in the softness of Pondicherry, dusky French citadel
placed among flowering forests: they are not taut and castaneted like
Salamanca, Cordoba, and the herb-scented Tarragona, nor nostalgic
as those dethroned jazz metropolises, Alabama and Dixie, nor screaming
and steely as Detroit; they do not offer the swooning languor of Vienna;
the barbarian, but fascinating, fur-clad clamour of the markets of
Nijni-Novgorod; the brocaded beauty of Ispahan, or the tinkling,
creole music of Louisiana . . . for these . . . Piacenza . . . Cremona
. . . Guastalla . . . Mirandola . . . Carpi . . . Crevalcore . . .
Gonzaga . . . Concordia, are names to be lingered over, mysterious
and harmonious, wrapped in the half-light of a history that cannot
quite be recalled; names to be rolled on the tongue, not ejaculated like

Cracow or München . . . flowers of European civilization, filling the mind of him who hears them with the sequent echoes of pealing bells and the brave clangour of trumpets.

Sir Osbert Sitwell

Norway's Fjords

IT WAS A lovely summer's day when I looked from my verandah over the fjord and drank my morning coffee in my pyjamas. Cultivated fields occasionally led down to the water's edge where several islands jettied into the lake, but the slopes were mostly wooded or cloaked with clumps of fir. Both shores met in the mid-distance where the tortuous waters seemed to be blocked by brown foothills which were topped by forests, hazy blue in the distance, which led up to grey mountains, their summits shining in the everlasting snow.

In such peaceful scenes I spent a lazy Sunday paddling about in a row-boat or loafing in the flower-scented garden while the inhabitants, who had donned their native costumes in honour of the visiting ship, relapsed into shorts, flannels, and sleeveless cotton frocks. Travelling north by steamer to Trondjheim one is soon introduced to what is the more typical scenery of Norway; a recurrent view of one of the deeper fjords may be described as a vista of grim precipitous cliff rising straight from depths, often half a mile down. But the lights and reflections in unruffled waters add romance to the sadness of harsh rock and dark forest.

On the left may lie a perpendicular black cliff which is mirrored in the water as polished malachite, while the rest of the fjord is pale blue with faint reflections of less severe hills on the opposite shore. In the distance where the two shores seem to meet, but actually wind away to the left, appears a sugarloaf hill, a truncated cone of a grey stone, which seems to be ubiquitous, and from the cliffs which partially conceal it, several waterfalls tumble, spreading into glistening spray and often making special rainbows by prismatic magic; and crowning this manifestation of the magnificence of mountain are the snow-clad peaks shining against an unclouded sky. Such is the scene to delight the eye of the most jaded traveller, but it is beyond description to portray the horrid forms and weird reverberating sounds with which these same jagged mountains may fill the valleys on a wild winter's night.

H. Muir Evans

North Labrador

A LAND of leaning ice
Hugged by plaster-grey arches of sky,
Flings itself silently
Into eternity.

" Has no one come here to win you,
Or left you with the faintest blush
Upon your glittering breasts?
Have you no memories, O Darkly Bright?"

Cold-hushed, there is only the shifting of moments
That journey toward no Spring—
No birth, no death, no time nor sun
In answer.

Hart Crane

Hebrides Hospitality

THE WEATHER was next day too violent for the continuation of our journey; but we had no reason to complain of the interruption. We saw in every place, what we chiefly desired to know, the manners of the people. We had company, and, if we had chosen retirement, we might have had books.

I never was in any house of the Islands, where I did not find books in more languages than one, if I staid long enough to want them, except one from which the family was removed. Literature is not neglected by the higher rank of the Hebridians.

It need not, I suppose, be mentioned, that in countries so little frequented as the Islands, there are no houses where travellers are entertained for money. He that wanders about these wilds, either procures recommendations to those whose habitations lie near his way, or, when night and weariness come upon him, takes the chance of general hospitality. If he finds only a cottage, he can expect little more than shelter; for the cottagers have little more for themselves: but if his good fortune brings him to the residence of a gentleman, he will be glad of a storm to prolong his stay. There is, however, one inn by the sea-side at Sconsor, in Sky, where the post-office is kept.

PLACES

At the tables where a stranger is received, neither plenty nor delicacy is wanting. A tract of land so thinly inhabited, must have much wildfowl; and I scarcely remember to have seen a dinner without them. The moorgame is everywhere to be had. That the sea abounds with fish, needs not be told, for it supplies a great part of Europe. The Isle of Sky has stags and roebucks, but no hares. They sell very numerous droves of oxen yearly to England, and therefore cannot be supposed to want beef at home. Sheep and goats are in great numbers, and they have the common domestick fowls.

But as there is nothing to be bought, every family must kill its own meat, and roast part of it somewhat sooner than Apicius would prescribe. Every kind of flesh is undoubtedly excelled by the variety and emulation of English markets; but that which is not best may be yet very far from bad, and he that shall complain of his fare in the Hebrides, has improved his delicacy more than his manhood.

Samuel Johnson

In Romney Marsh

As I WENT down to Dymchurch Wall,
 I heard the South sing o'er the land;
I saw the yellow sunlight fall
 On knolls where Norman churches stand.

And ringing shrilly, taut and lithe,
 Within the wind a core of sound,
The wire from Romney town to Hythe
 Alone its airy journey wound.

A veil of purple vapour flowed
 And trailed its fringe along the Straits;
The upper air like sapphire glowed;
 And roses filled Heaven's central gates.

Masts in the offing wagged their tops;
 The swinging waves pealed on the shore;
The saffron beach, all diamond drops
 And beads of surge, prolonged the roar.

117

As I came up from Dymchurch Wall,
  I saw above the Downs' low crest
The crimson brands of sunset fall,
  Flicker and fade from out the west.

Night sank: like flakes of silver fire
  The stars in one great shower came down;
Shrill blew the wind; and shrill the wire
  Rang out from Hythe to Romney town.

The darkly shining salt sea drops
  Streamed as the waves clashed on the shore;
The beach, with all its organ stops
  Pealing again, prolonged the roar.

John Davidson

The Gardens of Hohenheim

THE ROAD from Stuttgart to Hohenheim is, in some measure, an embodied history of the art of gardening, which offers to the attentive observer an interesting commentary. In the orchards, vineyards, and kitchen-gardens, past which the high road stretches, the first natural beginning of the garden-art is revealed to him, stripped of all æsthetic ornament. But now the French style of gardening greets him with dignified formality beneath the gaunt and abrupt walls of poplar, which unite the open landscape with Hohenheim and arouse expectation by their well-balanced form. This solemn impression rises to an almost painful intensity, as you roam through the chambers of the ducal palace, which for splendour and elegance has few peers, and in a certain rare manner combines taste with profusion. By the brilliance which here strikes the eye from every side, and by the exquisite architecture of the rooms and furniture, the craving for simplicity is wrought to the highest pitch, and the most conspicuous triumph is in waiting for rural Nature, which all at once welcomes the traveller into the so-called English Park. . . .

It is a Nature quickened with soul and exalted by art, which satisfies not only the man of simple taste, but also the spoiled child of culture, charming the one into reflection, and leading back the other to emotion.

Friedrich Schiller

Of Greatham

FOR PEACE, than knowledge more desirable,
Into your Sussex quietness I came,
When summer's green and gold and azure fell
Over the world in flame.

And peace upon your pasture-lands I found,
Where grazing flocks drift on continually,
As little clouds that travel with no sound
Across a windless sky.

Out of your oaks the birds call to their mates
That brood among the pines, where hidden deep
From curious eyes a world's adventure waits
In columned choirs of sleep.

Under the calm ascension of the night
We heard the mellow lapsing and return
Of night-owls purring in their groundling flight
Through lanes of darkling fern.

Unbroken peace when all the stars were drawn
Back to their lairs of light, and ranked along
From shire to shire the downs out of the dawn
Were risen in golden song.

I sing of peace who have known the large unrest
Of men bewildered in their travelling,
And I have known the bridal earth unblest
By the brigades of spring.

I have known that loss. And now the broken thought
Of nations marketing in death I know,
The very winds to threnodies are wrought
That on your downlands blow.

I sing of peace. Was it but yesterday
I came among your roses and your corn?
Then momently amid this wrath I pray
For yesterday reborn.

John Drinkwater

Champlain's Account of the Gougou

THERE IS still one strange thing, worthy of an account, which many savages have assured me was true; that is, that near the Bay of Heat, toward the south, there is an island where a frightful monster makes his home, which the savages call Gougou, and which they told me had the form of a woman, but very terrible, and of such a size that they told me the tops of the masts of our vessel would not reach to his waist, so great do they represent him; and they say that he has often eaten up and still continues to eat up many savages; these he puts, when he can catch them, into a great pocket, and afterwards he eats them; and those who had escaped the danger of this awful beast said that its pocket was so great that it could have put our vessel into it. This monster makes horrible noises in this island, which the savages call the Gougou; and when they speak of it, it is with unutterable fear, and several have assured me that they have seen him.

Even the above-mentioned Sieur Prèvert from St. Malo told me that, while going in search of mines, as mentioned in the preceding chapter, he passed so near the haunt of this terrible beast, that he and all those on board his vessel heard strange hissings from the noise she made, and that the savages with him told him it was the same creature, and that they were so afraid that they hid themselves wherever they could, for fear that she would come and carry them off. What makes me believe what they say is the fact that all the savages in general fear her, and tell such strange things of her that, if I were to record all they say of her, it would be considered as idle tales, but I hold that this is the dwelling-place of some devil that torments them in the manner described. This is what I have learned about this Gougou.

Samuel de Champlain

The Other England

ANYONE WHO goes to America with the good old British prejudice that there is nothing like England is due for some pleasant shocks. No part of the world was so aptly named as New England, and I am not the first Englishman to have travelled through the lovely countryside of Massachusetts, Vermont and New Hampshire with a queer feeling of inverted homesickness. There is green, rich altogether lovely country just north of Boston that continually reminded me of the best of England. The deep-wooded, shallow-streamed valleys of the White Mountains recalled the Valley of the Exe; the woods of Massachusetts are very like the woods of the English south country. But the real New England is probably in the villages: the white painted eighteenth-century houses standing back from the streets behind green lawns and weeping New England elms, the lovely, severe white Unitarian churches, the village green where the band plays on summer evenings.

Apart from this placid and rather homely kind of countryside, extremely beautiful though it is, New England can offer a good deal more. The lakes with dreamy Indian names are a sailing paradise: there is good climbing all along the Washington Range, where the mountains too are Indian-named, and in June there will still be ten or fifteen feet of snow in the famous Tuckermann Ravine. In June too the flowers are lovely: the huge magenta and white Indian roses, flaming stretches of Indian Paint Brush, pale blue geraniums, wild yellow-and-crimson aquilegia (*A. canadensis*), miles of honeysuckle, and best of all the huge pink, white and sometimes yellow lady-slippers. All these are roadside flowers. There are alpines on Washington. But the best of the country is felt in its huge unspoilt expanse of natural beauty. Unlike the English countryside, very little of it is man-made. From the top of Mount Manadnock I looked down on a stretch of lake and forest that cannot have changed much in two hundred years. A lean, sardonic, tired forest-ranger, whose wife had disturbed him a little by falling off the mountain that morning, saw me looking. His words are the best recommendation of an entrancing countryside.

" Yeh, brother," he said, " it gets you."

H. E. Bates

The Slave Pens of Cape Lopez

CAPE LOPEZ boasts of two slave-factories. I now visited the one kept by the Portuguese. It was, from the outside, an immense enclosure, protected by a fence of palisades twelve feet high, and sharp-pointed at the top. Passing through the gate, which was standing open, I found myself in the midst of a large collection of shanties surrounded by shade-trees, under which were lying about, in various positions, people enough to form a considerable African town.

An old Portuguese, who seemed to be sick, met and welcomed me, and conducted me to the white men's house, a two-storey frame building, which stood immediately fronting the gate. This was poorly furnished, but contained beds, a table, chairs, etc.

Unfortunately I do not speak either Spanish or Portuguese, and my conductor understood neither French nor English. We had, therefore, to make use of a native interpreter, who made slow work of our talk. The Portuguese complained that it was now very hard to land a cargo in the Brazils, as the Government was against them, and that each year the trade grew duller. To put myself on a right footing with him, I told him I had not come to trade, but to collect objects in natural history, and to see the country and hunt.

I was now led around. The large house I have mentioned was surrounded by a separate strong fence, and in the spacious yard which was thus cut off were the male slaves, fastened six together by a little stout chain which passed through a collar secured about the neck of each. This mode of fastening experience has proved to be the most secure. It is rare that six men are unanimous in any move for their own good, and it is found that no attempts to liberate themselves, when thus fastened, succeed. They reposed under sheds or shelters built about the yard, and here and there were buckets of water from which they could drink when they felt inclined.

Beyond this yard was another for the women and children, who were not manacled, but allowed to rove at pleasure through their yard, which was also protected by a fence. The men were almost naked. The women wore invariably a cloth about their middle.

Behind the great houses was the hospital for sick slaves. It was not ill-arranged, the rooms being large and well-ventilated, and the beds —structures of bamboo covered with a mat—were ranged about the walls.

Outside of all the minor yards, under some trees, were the huge cauldrons in which the beans and rice, which serve as slave-food, were cooked. Each yard had several Portuguese overseers, who kept watch and order, and superintended the cleaning out of the yards, which is performed daily by the slaves themselves. From time to time, too, these overseers take the slaves down to the seashore and make them bathe.

I remarked that many of the slaves were quite merry, and seemed perfectly content with their fate. Others were sad, and seemed filled with dread of their future; for, to lend an added horror to the position of these poor creatures, they firmly believe that we whites buy them to eat them. They cannot conceive of any other use to be made of them; and wherever the slave-trade is known in the interior, it is believed that the white men beyond sea are great cannibals, who have to import blacks for the market. Thus a chief in the interior country, having a great respect for me, of whom he had often heard, when I made him my first visit, immediately ordered a slave to be killed for my dinner, and it was only with great difficulty I was able to convince him that I did not, in my own country, live on human flesh.

Paul B. du Chaillu

Desert Day

THE SUMMER'S night at end, the sun stands up as a crown of hostile flames from that huge covert of inhospitable sandstone bergs; the desert day dawns not little and little, but it is noon-tide in an hour. The sun, entering as a tyrant upon the waste landscape, darts upon us a torment of fiery beams, not to be remitted till the far-off evening. No matins here of birds; not a rock partridge-cock, calling with blithesome chuckle over the extreme waterless desolation. Grave is that giddy heat upon the crown of the head; the ears tingle with a flickering shrillness, a subtle crepitation it seems, in the glassiness of this sun-stricken nature: the hot sand-blink is in the eyes, and there is little refreshment to find in the tents' shelter; the worsted booths leak to this fiery rain of sunny light. Mountains looming like dry bones through the thin air, stand far around about us: the savage flank of Ybba Moghrair, the high spire and ruinous stacks of el-Jebâl, Chebàd, the coast of Helwàn!

Herds of weak nomad camels waver dispersedly, seeking pasture in the midst of this hollow fainting country, where but lately the swarming locusts have fretted every green thing. This silent air burning about us, we endure breathless till the *assr*: when the dozing Arabs in the tents revive after their heavy hours. The lingering day draws down to the sun-setting; the herdsmen, weary of the sun, come again with the cattle, to taste in their *menzils* the first sweetness of mirth and repose. The day is done, and there rises the nightly freshness of this purest mountain air: and then to the cheerful song and the cup at the common fire. The moon rises ruddy from that solemn obscurity of *jebel* like a mighty beacon:—and the morrow will be as this day, days deadly drowned in the sun of the summer wilderness.

Charles M. Doughty

Arabia

FAR ARE the shades of Arabia,
 Where the Princes ride at noon,
'Mid the verdurous vales and thickets,
 Under the ghost of the moon;
And so dark is that vaulted purple,
 Flowers in the forest rise
And toss into blossom 'gainst the phantom stars
 Pale in the noonday skies.

Sweet is the music of Arabia
 In my heart, when out of dreams
I still in the thin clear mirk of dawn
 Descry her gliding streams;
Hear her strange lutes on the green banks
 Ring loud with the grief and delight
Of the dim-silked, dark-haired Musicians
 In the brooding silence of night.

They haunt me—her lutes and her forests;
 No beauty on earth I see
But shadowed with that dream recalls
 Her loveliness to me:
Still eyes look coldly upon me,
 Cold voices whisper and say—
" He is crazed with the spell of far Arabia,
 They have stolen his wits away."

Walter de la Mare

A House in the Tyrol

THE SUN was strong and golden and warm, but the breeze that was soughing through the pine-woods and swinging the bright green plumes of the larches to and fro had the crispness of snow in it as I set off one afternoon along the lake road from Pertisau to Eben.

Apple-trees in bloom stood silver-white in the flowery meadows round an ancient farmhouse on the roof of which small grey boulders had been strewn to keep the shingles down. Behind the house the brilliant green slope had a bubbled surface like the crust of boiling paint. A curious but lovely effect. And above the turbulent green of the slope the pine-forest clothed the mountain side in mysterious gloom. As I passed, an old woman in a gentian-blue apron with a white head kerchief tied under her chin came to the door of the barn (which is joined to the back of the farmhouse) and from the dark behind her sounded the feeble complaint of a new-born calf.

I do not think in all Tyrol I saw a house more lovable than that one. There were grander houses but none to speak more clearly of quiet dignity and beauty and tradition and gentle faith and labour and simple gaiety, and all that one comes in the end to connect with the Tyrolese country people. Its upper storey was of grey weather-board, the lower brilliantly whitewashed. From the side on account of the barn it was a much bigger house than seen from the front. On the white front wall were the fresco of a saint and a verse praying God and the saint to watch over the house and keep from it all evil and all enemies, both of man and beast. The fresco was scarcely to be made out so faded it had become, but the Gothic lettering of the prayer was so richly black I think it had but lately been done over. There was no spacing between the words. They must have been written like that, running into each other, since the house was built four hundred years ago. The dark wooden balcony, fretted at the edge in an openwork design and running the full length of the front, was gay with the crimson and gold of begonias in pots, and above it right under the eaves a second tiny carved wooden balcony opened off an attic, in the dusk of which you could make out the harness of the farm-horses hanging from the rafters.

Before a Tyrolese peasant-house one's mind slips back to the old folk-tales of beasts that talked with men. For here obviously the home is as much a shelter for the animals as for their masters, and you feel that living in such close proximity a special sort of under-standing must spring up between the beasts and those who cherish them with such solicitude. In winter, even the fowls have their place indoors. Low down in the wall you will notice the hole cut for their entry into the kitchen. Behind the kitchen is the stable, divided into compartments where the horses, the cows, the pigs, stay snug while the countryside is white with snow. Above them is the hayloft. In the master's quarters the living-room is sacred, but into the sleeping-rooms the farm penetrates in the shape of bits of harness and field implements and all kinds of odds and ends for storing.

When winter howls at the door there must be a really dramatic sense of satisfaction in knowing all one's possessions to be under the roof with oneself. Only the firewood is left actually out of doors. Yet it hugs the wall so close in golden-brown stacks under the shelter of the balconies, it too seems to have been admitted to the friendly alliance of man and beast.

Nina Murdoch

The Apennines

LISTEN, listen, Mary mine,
To the whisper of the Apennine,
It bursts on the roof like the thunder's roar,
Or like the sea on a northern shore,
Heard in its raging ebb and flow
By the captives pent in the cave below.
The Apennine in the light of day
Is a mighty mountain dim and gray,
Which between the earth and sky doth lay;
But when night comes, a chaos dread
On the dim starlight then is spread,
And the Apennine walks abroad with the storm,
Shrouding. . . .

Percy Bysshe Shelley

The Spell of the Shetlands

SEE THE Shetlands once, and they will haunt you for ever. They are mad little islands, like a mountain range sunk below its timber line, forming a teeth of rocks between the Atlantic and the North Sea. There is not a spot in the whole hundred of them that is more than half a mile from salt water.

Their coast line is crazy. It is a sort of geologic debauch where the rocks have gone mad indeed. They shoot out of the sea in sheer cliffs—Foula's Atlantic side is one sheer cliff 1300 feet high. They used to pitch their dead " over the Sneug ". They called it a burial, as they had not enough earth to inter a corpse. The people of Foula used to live on just fish and guillemot's eggs (which bird to oblige them lays a lopsided egg that won't roll off a rocky ledge); and if you go off to Foula in the mail boat, you may not be able to get back for weeks. The islands along the Atlantic coast are often just spear-points of red rock. There are rock arches through which one could sail a full-rigged sailing ship. The Atlantic rushes up to them, flings itself high up their sides and falls back in a lacery of white, broken seas. Spotted seals bask and call on the fantastic red shelves. The great whale blows off shore. Gannets, guillemots, fulmar petrels, shags and puffins scream from the serrated ledges of the cliffs, shoot past in staring flotillas on the tide and whirl in a feathered spray over the endless waves. For six hours each day the Atlantic sets through the Shetlands, sweeping in great swirling eddies to bring the flood tide. Then it ebbs, and the North Sea races after it, leaping and thrumming through the rips of Yell and Blue Mull Sound, so that even the connecting motor-boat has to fight to win the other side.

But inland all is monotony. Black peat, bogs and long lonely moors. A sheep is visible on the sky-line for miles. There are no real streams, only gurgling burns, which run almost unseen through the black channels they have dug among the peat, to empty into shallow wind-swept lochs, where the water lies black as coffee; and the lonely cry of the curlew is the only sound as you moodily cast your flies for the speckled Shetland trout.

. . . They are lonely and dreary little islands; they are windswept and battered; and yet, if you have stood on their wine-red moors at sunset and seen the great swells of the Atlantic pounding in, you will never forget them.

Negley Farson

Gibraltar

ENGLAND, we love thee better than we know.—
    And this I learn'd when, after wand'rings long
    'Mid people of another stock and tongue,
I heard again thy martial music blow,
And saw thy gallant children to and fro
    Pace, keeping ward at one of those huge gates,
    Twin giants watching the Herculean Straits.
When first I came in sight of that brave show,
    It made the very heart within me dance,
    To think that thou thy proud foot should'st advance

Forward so far into the mighty sea.
Joy was it and exultation to behold
Thine ancient standard's rich emblazonry,
A glorious picture by the wind unroll'd.

Richard Chenevix Trench

A Town in Spain

THERE IS a town in Spain called Querinda. You will not find it upon the map: it is an unimportant, forgotten place visited only by those who have lost their way—and inhabited, according to most visitors, by those who have lost their reason.

In appearance Querinda is exquisite but haphazard, its avenues being, for the most part, winding lanes, and the principal square an oblong. The town statues represent, in extremely dramatic attitudes, nobody in particular. The chief clock—much to the confusion of those who have motor-buses or posts to catch—gives a different time from any other clock in Spain. There is no railway service; one arrives by road and by accident.

The large untidy church which dominates Querinda, tumbled perilously on the river bank, has an inexplicable chimney stack for which not even the ingenious natives of the place have ever been able to give an adequate history. There is no fireplace inside. One has to accept the chimney as a natural phenomenon, and agree that the church must have flung it up in a moment of boredom.

The inhabitants of this peculiar place are a vague happy people who celebrate more holidays than anybody else; for the locality, they say, was uncommonly rich in saints. They take no pains to encourage other produce, and are out of touch with places that are out of sight. The news of Querinda itself is to be learnt only from a town crier, whose voice grows thicker in proportion to the number of inns he passes. Naturally, there is little of law or order in such a place, but the rest of Spain does not mind since it does not know, and so all are content.

Querinda is at its best of a late summer morning, when half the market-place is blue-shadowed by the large grey church, and there are men like pirates helping up their treasure of fruit—green figs, water-melons and muscatels—and sturdy women spreading their kerchiefs in the sun. There are children agape at the old fountain, while a stone man flings high into the air diamonds, and, as they fall, catches them. He has clear pools like mirrors to guard; and when the little giggling laundresses come with their baskets of linen, he tells them how beautiful they are growing. He remembers all the secrets that they cannot keep, and he remembers the boy Luis, who ran away with soldiers to the parched African desert and died there dreaming of him.

Sometimes in the morning there comes the strange last outpost of Africa, with leather pouches and slippers and stories to sell. One would not expect to find him so far north: he has the air of an old man lost. Yet on market-day he draws many coppers with an old tale of San Eugenio that everybody knows. He is a wrinkled, shiny little Moor, troubled by flies and the mockery of children. Laughter always follows as his yellow slippers go flapping round the square.

Between lunch and the evening meal—the Spanish afternoon of seven or eight hours during which energetic visitors madly long for something to happen—Querinda spends some time in sleep. Not that the men retire to walled gardens of green balconies, emptying the streets and public places: they seem to fall asleep wherever they happen to be, whatever they happen to be doing, as though a spell has been suddenly cast upon them. There is not a woman to be seen. But on doorsteps, under trees, over benches, beside walls, against statues, on the brink of fountains, and even upon the pavement, lie men of all ages and descriptions in attitudes of lazy content. Not a sound, not a movement, not a gesture to drive the flies away. For some hours they sprawl, swarthy old men and fine boys, their hands still clasping a half-eaten apple, a newspaper, a driver's whip, an empty bottle.

From three to five, as the air changes from gold to silver, the whole town lolls. From five to seven, as the sun begins to deepen the red of roofs, figures here and there are stirring, stretching, yawning, and thinking of going about their business. From seven to nine they go. For, of course, if one does no work at all, one is not paid. And if one is not paid, one cannot buy food or wine or go to the bullfight.

During the summer there are bullfights on Sundays at five o'clock—by Querinda time, of course. Toreros come over from Pontevedra or some such place, and all the girls of Querinda put on bright stockings and shawls; and sometimes they carry flowers to throw to a bullfighter in the hope that he will follow them home and stand under their windows. Which has been known to happen. The bullfight in Querinda is never as bullfights are elsewhere—one would scarcely expect that. A bull usually escapes from the sanded ring and knocks over the lemonade stall. Everybody shouts and the women faint in becoming attitudes. And the next day there is a subscription for the owner of the lemonade stall, who finds the whole business rather profitable.

Anthony Thorne

Rue de la Gaieté

THE RUE DE LA GAIETÉ overflows at one end into an open-air market of vegetables and flowers, and sometimes, as today, of singing birds, poultry, and brooding families of cats. Should the passer-by cast so much as an eye upon these, he falls into the toils of the market-people. They press the cats to their bosoms, extolling their probity, their cleanliness, their race; each has been in its turn the happiness, the day-star, of some lonely hearth, but to Madame they will sacrifice their treasure for ten francs. Madame remains unmoved, and they fling aside the domestic treasures and snatch the birds out of their cages; they bring out more cages, and yet more birds. They hurl these aside in their turn, and unearth crates of seemingly moribund tortoises; so that the victim, weakened by seeing what huge trouble has been taken on her account, finally falls, and possibly embitters her future life by the purchase of a tortoise.

E. Œ. Somerville and Martin Ross

The Englishman in Italy

. . . OH, HEAVEN and the terrible crystal!
   No rampart excludes
Your eye from the life to be lived
   In the blue solitudes.
Oh, those mountains, their infinite movement!
   Still moving with you;
For, ever some new head and breast of them
   Thrusts into view
To observe the intruder; you see it
   If quickly you turn
And, before they escape you surprise them.
   They grudge you should learn
How the soft plains they look on, lean over
   And love (they pretend)

—Cower beneath them, the flat sea-pine crouches,
   The wild fruit-trees bend,
E'en the myrtle-leaves curl, shrink and shut:
   All is silent and grave:
'Tis a sensual and timorous beauty,
   How fair! but a slave.
So, I turned to the sea; and there slumbered
   As greenly as ever
Those isles of the siren, your Galli;
   No ages can sever
The Three, nor enable their sister
   To join them,—halfway
On the voyage, she looked at Ulysses—
   No farther today,
Tho' the small one, just launched in the wave
   Watches breast-high and steady
From under the rock, her bold sister
   Swum halfway already.
Fortù, shall we sail there together
   And see from the sides
Quite new rocks show their faces, new haunts
   Where the siren abides?
Shall we sail round and round them, close over
   The rocks, tho' unseen,
That ruffle the grey glassy water
   To glorious green?
Then scramble from splinter to splinter,
   Reach land and explore,
On the largest, the strange square black turret
   With never a door,
Just a loop to admit the quick lizards;
   Then, stand there and hear
The birds' quiet singing, that tells us
   What life is, so clear?
—The secret they sang to Ulysses
   When, ages ago,
He heard and he knew this life's secret
   I hear and I know.

Robert Browning

Nicolo Zeno in Engroneland, 1380

M. NICOLO remaining now in Bres determined in the spring to go forth and discover land: wherefore arming out three small barks in the month of July, he sailed to the northwards and arrived in Engroneland. Where he found a monastery of friars of the order of the Predicators, and a church dedicated to Saint Thomas, hard by a hill that casteth forth fire like Vesuvius and Etna.

There is a fountain of hot burning water with the which they heat the church of the monastery and the friars' chambers; it cometh also into the kitchen so boiling hot that they use no other fire to dress their meat: and putting their bread into brass pots without any water, it doth bake it as it were in an hot oven. They have also small gardens covered over in the winter time, which being watered with this water, are defended from the force of the snow and cold, which in those parts being situate far under the pole, is very extreme, and by this means they produce flowers and fruits and herbs of sundry sorts, even as in other temperate countries in their seasons, in such sort that the rude and savage people of those parts seeing these supernatural effects, do take those friars for gods, and bring them many presents, as chickens, flesh and divers other things, and have them all in great reverence as lords. When the frost and snow is great they heat their houses in manner beforesaid, and will by letting in the water or opening the windows at an instant temper the heat and cold at their pleasure.

Richard Hakluyt

Majorca

I HAVE never seen anything so bright, and at the same time so melancholy, as these perspectives where the ilex, the carob, pine, olive, poplar, and cypress mingle their various hues in the hollows of the mountain-abysses of verdure, where the torrent precipitates its course under mounds of sumptuous richness and inimitable grace . . .

While you hear the sound of the sea on the northern coast, you perceive it only as a faint shining line beyond the sinking mountains and the great plain which is unrolled to the southward—a sublime picture, framed in the foreground by dark rocks covered with pines; in the middle distance by mountains of boldest outline, fringed with superb trees, and beyond these by rounded hills which the setting sun gilds with burning colours, where the eye distinguishes, a league away, the microscopic profile of trees, fine as the antennæ of butterflies, black and clear as pen-drawings of Indian ink on a ground of sparkling gold. It is one of those landscapes which oppress you because they leave nothing to be desired, nothing to be imagined. Nature has here created that which the poet and the painter behold in their dreams. An immense ensemble, infinite details, inexhaustible variety, blended forms, sharp contours, dim, vanishing depths—all are present, and art can suggest nothing further. Majorca is one of the most beautiful countries in the world for the painter, and one of the least known. It is a green Helvetia under the sky of Calabria, with the solemnity and silence of the Orient.

George Sand

The East

AND THIS is how I see the East. I have seen its secret places and have looked into its very soul; but now I see it always from a small boat, a high outline of mountains, blue and afar in the morning; like faint mist at noon; a jagged wall of purple at sunset. I have the feel of the oar in my hand, the vision of a scorching blue sea in my eyes. And I see a bay, a wide bay, smooth as glass and polished like ice, shimmering in the dark. A red light burns far off upon the gloom of the land, and the night is soft and warm. We drag at the oars with aching arms, and suddenly a puff of wind, a puff faint and tepid and laden with strange odours of blossoms, of aromatic wood, comes out of the still night—the first sigh of the East on my face. That I can never forget. It was impalpable and enslaving, like a charm, like a whispered promise of mysterious delight.

. . . I pulled back, made fast again to the jetty, and then went to sleep at last. I had faced the silence of the East. I had heard some of its language. But when I opened my eyes again the silence was as complete as though it had never been broken. I was lying in a flood of light, and the sky had never looked so far, so high, before. I opened my eyes and lay without moving.

And then I saw the men of the East—they were looking at me. The whole length of the jetty was full of people. I saw brown, bronze, yellow faces, the black eyes, the glitter, the colour of an Eastern crowd. And all these beings stared without a murmur, without a sigh, without a movement. They stared down at the boats, at the sleeping men who at night had come to them from the sea. Nothing moved. The fronds of palms stood still against the sky. Not a branch stirred along the shore, and the brown roofs of hidden houses peeped through the green foliage, through the big leaves that hung shining and still like leaves forged of heavy metal. This was the East of the ancient navigators, so old, so mysterious, resplendent and sombre, living and unchanged, full of danger and promise. And these were the men.

Joseph Conrad

Tarantella

Do you remember an inn,
Miranda?
Do you remember an Inn?
And the tedding and the spreading
Of the straw for a bedding,
And the fleas that tease in the High Pyrenees,
And the wine that tasted of the tar?
And the cheers and the jeers of the young muleteers
(Under the dark of the vine verandah)?

Do you remember an Inn, Miranda,
Do you remember an Inn?
And the cheers and the jeers of the young muleteers
Who hadn't got a penny,
And who weren't paying any,
And the hammer at the doors and the Din?
And the Hip! Hop! Hap!
Of the clap
Of the hands to the twirl and the swirl
Of the girl gone chancing,
Glancing,
Dancing,
Backing and advancing,
Snapping of the clapper to the spin
Out and in—
And the Ting, Tong, Tang of the guitar!
Do you remember an Inn,
Miranda?
Do you remember an Inn?

Never more;
Miranda,
Never more,
Only the high peaks hoar:
And Aragon a torrent at the door.
No sound
In the walls of the Halls where falls
The tread
Of the feet of the dead to the ground.
No sound:
Only the boom
Of the far Waterfall like Doom.

Hilaire Belloc

On Horseback in Andalusia

I KNOW of few things in this life more delicious than a ride in the spring or summer season in the neighbourhood of Seville. . . .

It is here that the balmy air of beautiful Andalusia is to be inhaled in full perfection. Aromatic herbs and flowers are growing in abundance, diffusing their perfume around. Here dark and gloomy cares are dispelled as if by magic from the bosom, as the eyes wander over the prospect, lighted by unequalled sunshine, in which gaily painted butterflies wanton, and green and golden salamanquesas lie extended, enjoying the luxurious warmth, and occasionally startling the traveller by springing up and making off with portentous speed to the nearest coverts, whence they stare upon him with their sharp and lustrous eyes . . .

Every evening it was my custom to ride along the Dehesa, until the topmost towers of Seville were no longer in sight. I then turned about, and pressing my knees against the sides of Sidi Habismilk, my Arabian, the fleet creature, to whom spur or lash had never been applied, would set off in the direction of the town with the speed of a whirlwind, seeming in his headlong course to devour the ground of the waste, until he had left it behind, then dashing through the elm-covered road of the Delicias, his thundering hoofs were soon heard beneath the vaulted archway of the Puerta de Xeres, and in another moment he would stand stone-still before the door of my solitary house in the little silent square of the Pila Seca.

George Borrow

Grantchester

AH GOD! to see the branches stir
Across the moon at Grantchester!
To smell the thrilling-sweet and rotten,
Unforgettable, unforgotten
River smell, and hear the breeze
Sobbing in the little trees.
Say, do the elm-clumps greatly stand,
Still guardians of that holy land?
The chestnuts shade, in reverend dream,
The yet unacademic stream?
Is dawn a secret shy and cold
Anadyomene, silver-gold?
And sunset still a golden sea
From Haslingfield to Madingley?
And after, ere the night is born,
Do hares come out about the corn?
Oh, is the water sweet and cool,
Gentle and brown, above the pool?
And laughs the immortal river still
Under the mill, under the mill?
Say, is there Beauty yet to find?
And Certainty? and Quiet kind?
Deep meadows yet, for to forget
The lies, the truths, and pain? . . . oh! yet
Stands the Church clock at ten-to-three?
And is there honey still for tea?

Rupert Brooke

Tahiti

TAHITI IS by far the most famous island in the South Seas; indeed
a variety of causes has made it almost classic. Its natural features
alone distinguish it from the surrounding groups. Two round
and lofty promontories rise nine thousand feet above the level of
the ocean, are connected by a low, narrow isthmus; the whole being
some one hundred miles in circuit. From the great central peaks

of the larger peninsula—Orohena, Aorai, and Pirohitee—the land radiates on all sides to the sea in sloping green ridges. Between these are broad and shadowy valleys—in aspect, each a Tempee—watered with fine streams, and thickly wooded. Unlike many of the other islands, there extends nearly all round Tahiti a belt of low, alluvial soil teeming with the richest vegetation. Here, chiefly, the natives dwell.

Seen from the sea the prospect is magnificent. It is one mass of shaded tints of green from beach to mountain-top; endlessly diversified with valleys, ridges, glens, and cascades. Over the ridges, here and there, the loftier peaks fling their shadows, and far down the valleys. At the head of these, the waterfalls flash out into the sunlight as if pouring through vertical bowers of verdure. Such enchantment, too, breathes over the whole, that it seems a fairy world, all fresh and blooming from the Creator.

Upon a near approach the picture loses not its attractions. It is no exaggeration to say that to a European of any sensibility, who for the first time wanders into these valleys—away from the haunts of the natives—the ineffable repose and beauty of the landscape is such, that every object strikes him like something seen in a dream; and for a time he almost refuses to believe that scenes like these should have a commonplace existence.

Herman Melville

The Isles of Greece

THE ISLES of Greece! the Isles of Greece!
   Where burning Sappho loved and sung,
Where grew the arts of War and Peace,
   Where Delos rose, and Phœbus sprung!
Eternal summer gilds them yet,
But all, except their Sun, is set.

The Scian and the Teian muse,
   The Hero's harp, the Lover's lute,
Have found the fame your shores refuse:
   Their place of birth alone is mute
To sounds which echo further west
Than your Sires' " Islands of the Blest ".

The mountains look on Marathon—
  And Marathon looks on the sea;
And musing there an hour alone,
  I dreamed that Greece might still be free;
For standing on the Persians' grave,
I could not deem myself a slave.

A King sate on the rocky brow
  Which looks o'er sea-born Salamis;
And ships, by thousands, lay below,
  And men in nations;—all were his!
He counted them at break of day—
And, when the Sun set, where were they?

And where are they? and where art thou,
  My Country? On thy voiceless shore
The heroic lay is tuneless now—
  The heroic bosom beats no more!
And must thy Lyre, so long divine,
Degenerate into hands like mine?

'Tis something, in the dearth of Fame,
  Though link'd among a fetter'd race,
To feel at least a patriot's shame,
  Even as I sing, suffuse my face;
For what is left the poet here?
For Greeks a blush—for Greece a tear.

                                    Lord Byron

Under the Equator

IN EUROPE, a woodland scene has its spring, its summer, its autumnal, and its winter aspects. In the equatorial forests the aspect is the same or nearly so every day in the year: budding, flowering, fruiting, and leaf-shedding are always going on in one species or other. The activity of birds and insects proceeds without interruption, each species having its own separate times; the colonies of wasps, for instance, do not die off annually, leaving only the queens, as in cold climates; but the succession of generations and colonies goes on incessantly. It is never either spring, summer, or autumn, but each day is a combination of all three. With the day and night always of equal length, the atmospheric disturbances of each day neutralizing themselves before each succeeding morn; with the sun in its course proceeding mid-way across the sky, and the daily temperature the same within two or three degrees throughout the year—how grand in its perfect equilibrium and simplicity is the march of Nature under the equator!

Henry Walter Bates

In Padua

LUCENTIO : Tranio, since for the great desire I had
To see fair Padua, nursery of arts,
I am arriv'd for fruitful Lombardy,
The pleasant garden of great Italy;
And by my father's love and leave am arm'd
With his good will and thy good company,
My trusty servant well approv'd in all,
Here let us breathe, and haply institute
A course of learning and ingenious studies.
Pisa, renowned for grave citizens,
Gave me my being and my father first,
A merchant of great traffic through the world,
Vincentio, come of the Bentivolii.
Vincentio's son, brought up in Florence,
It shall become to serve all hopes conceiv'd,
To deck his fortune with his virtuous deeds:
And therefore, Tranio, for the time I study,
Virtue and that part of philosophy
Will I apply that treats of happiness
By virtue specially to be achiev'd.
Tell me thy mind; for I have Pisa left
And am to Padua come, as he that leaves
A shallow plash to plunge him in the deep,
And with satiety seeks to quench his thirst.

TRANIO : *Mi perdonate*, gentle master mine,
I am in all affected as yourself,
Glad that you thus continue your resolve
To suck the sweets of sweet philosophy.

139

Only, good master, while we do admire
This virtue and this moral discipline,
Let's be no stoics nor no stocks, I pray;
Or so devote to Aristotle's checks
As Ovid be an outcast quite abjur'd.
Balk logic with acquaintance that you have,
And practise rhetoric in your common talk;
Music and poesy use to quicken you;
The mathematics and the metaphysics,
Fall to them as you find your stomach serves you;
No profit grows where is no pleasure ta'en;
In brief, sir, study what you most affect.

LUC. : Gramercies, Tranio, well dost thou advise.
If, Biondello, thou wert come ashore,
We could at once put us in readiness,
And take a lodging fit to entertain
Such friends as time in Padua shall beget.
But stay awhile: what company is this?

TRA. : Master, some show to welcome us to town.

William Shakespeare

The Bay of Rio

I HAVE said that I must pass over Rio without a description; but just now such a flood of scented reminiscences steals over me, that I must needs yield and recant, as I inhale that musky air.

More than one hundred and fifty miles' circuit of living green hills embosoms a translucent expanse, so hemmed in by sierras of grass, that among the Indian tribes the place was known as " The Hidden Water ". On all sides, in the distance, rise high conical peaks, which at sunrise burn like vast tapers; and down from the interior, through vineyards and forests, flow radiating streams, all emptying into the harbour.

Talk not of Bahia de Todos os Santos—the Bay of All Saints; for though that be a glorious haven, yet Rio is the Bay of all Rivers—the Bay of all Delights—the Bay of all Beauties. From circumjacent hill-sides, untiring summer hangs perpetually in terraces of vivid verdure; and, embossed with old mosses, convent and castle nestle in valley and glen.

All round, deep inlets run into the green mountain land, and, over-hung with wild Highlands, more resemble Loch Katrines than Lake Lemans. And though Loch Katrine has been sung by the bonneted Scott, and Lake Leman by the coroneted Byron; yet here, in Rio, both the loch and the lake are but two wild flowers in a prospect that is almost unlimited. For, behold! far away and away, stretches the broad blue of the water, to yonder soft-swelling hills of light green, backed by the purple pinnacles and pipes of the Grand Organ Moun-tains; fitly so called, for in thunder-time they roll cannonades down the bay, drowning the blended bass of all the cathedrals in Rio. Shout again, exalt your voices, stamp your feet, jubilate, Organ Mountains! and roll your Te Deums round the world.

What though, for more than five thousand five hundred years, this grand harbour of Rio lay hid in the hills, unknown by the Catholic Portuguese? Centuries before Haydn performed before emperors and kings, these Organ Mountains played his *Oratorio of the Creation*, before the Creator himself. But nervous Haydn could not have endured that cannonading choir, since this composer of thunderbolts himself died at last through the crashing commotion of Napoleon's bombard-ment of Vienna.

But all mountains are Organ Mountains: the Alps and the Himalayas; the Appalachian Chain, the Ural, the Andes, the Green Hills and the White. All of them play anthems for ever: *The Messiah*, and *Samson*, and *Israel in Egypt*, and *Saul*, and *Judas Maccabeus*, and *Solomon*.

Archipelago Rio! ere Noah on old Ararat anchored his ark, there lay anchored in you all these green rocky isles I now see. But God did not build on you, isles! those long lines of batteries; nor did our blessed Saviour stand godfather at the christening of yon frowning fortress of Santa Cruz, though named in honour of himself, the divine Prince of Peace!

Amphitheatrical Rio! in your vast expanse might be held the Resur-rection and Judgement Day of the whole world's men-of-war, re-presented by the flag-ships of fleets—the flag-ships of the Phoenician armed galleys of Tyre and Sidon; of King Solomon's annual squadron that sailed to Ophir; whence in after times, perhaps, sailed the Acapulco fleets of the Spaniards, with golden ingots for ballasting; the flag-ships of all the Greek and Persian craft that exchanged the war-hug at Salamis; of all the Roman and Egyptian galleys that, eagle-like, with blood-dripping brows, beaked each other at Actium; of all the Danish keels of the Vikings; of all the mosquito craft of Abba Thule, king of the Pelews, when he went to vanquish Artingall; of all the Venetian, Genoese, and Papal fleets that came to the shock at Lepanto; of both horns of the crescent of the Spanish Armada; of the Portuguese squadron that, under the gallant Gama, chastised the Moors, and discovered the Moluccas; of all the Dutch navies led by Van Tromp, and sunk by Admiral Hawke; of the forty-seven French and Spanish sail-of-the-line that, for three months, essayed to batter down Gibraltar; of all Nelson's seventy-fours that thunder-bolted off St. Vincent's, at the Nile, Copenhagen, and Trafalgar; of all the frigate-merchantmen of the East India Company; of Perry's war-brigs, sloops, and schooners that scattered the British armament on Lake Erie; of all the Barbary corsairs captured by Bainbridge; of all the war-canoes of the Polynesian kings, Tammamammaha and Pomare—aye! one and all, with Commodore Noah for their Lord High Admiral—in this abounding Bay of Rio these flag-ships might all come to anchor, and swing round in concert to the first of the flood.

Herman Melville

On Old Rome

HERE WAS old Rome that stretch'd her Empire far,
In Peace was fear'd, triumphant was in War:
Here 'twas, for now its place is only found,
All that was Rome lyes buried under Ground.

These Ruines hid in Weeds, on which Man treads,
Were Structures which to Heav'n rais'd their proud Heads:
Rome that subdu'd the World, to Time now yields,
With Rubbish swells the Plains, and strews the Fields.

Think not to see what so Renown'd has been,
Nothing of Rome, in Rome is to be seen;
Vulcan and Mars, those wasting Gods, have come,
And ta'en Rome's Greatness utterly from Rome.

They spoil'd with Malice, e'er they would depart,
What e'er was rare of Nature or of Art:
Its greatest Trophies they destroy'd and burn'd;
She that o'erturn'd the World, to Dust is turn'd.

Well might she fall, 'gainst whom such Foes conspire,
Old Time, Revengeful Man, and Sword and Fire:
Now all we see of the Great Empress Rome,
Are but the Sacred Reliques of her Tomb.

Philip Ayres

The River Clitumnus

HAVE YOU ever seen the source of the river Clitumnus? As I never
heard you mention it, I imagine not; let me therefore advise you
to do so immediately. It is but lately indeed I had that pleasure,
and I condemn myself for not having seen it sooner. At the foot
of a little hill, covered with venerable and shady cypress-trees, a
spring issues out, which gushing in different and unequal streams,
forms itself, after several windings, into a spacious bason, so extremely clear, that you may see the pebbles, and the little pieces of
money which are thrown into it, as they lie at the bottom. From thence
it is carried off not so much by the declivity of the ground, as by its
own strength and fullness.

It is navigable almost as soon as it has quitted its source, and wide
enough to admit a free passage for ships to pass by each other, as they
sail with or against the stream. The current runs so strong, tho' the
ground is level, that the vessels which go down the river have no
occasion to make use of their oars; while those which ascend, find it
difficult to advance, even with the assistance of oars and poles: and
this vicissitude of labour and ease, is exceedingly amusing when one
sails up and down merely for pleasure. The banks on each side are
shaded with the verdure of great numbers of ash and poplar trees, as
clearly and distinctly seen in the stream, as if they were actually sunk
in it. The water is cold as snow, and as white too. Near it stands an
ancient and venerable temple, wherein is placed the river-god Clitumnus clothed in a robe, whose immediate presence the prophetic
oracles here delivered, sufficiently testify. Several little chapels are
scattered round, dedicated to particular gods distinguished by different
names, and some of them too presiding over different fountains. For,
besides the principal one, which is, as it were, the parent of all the
rest, there are several lesser streams, which, taking their rise from
various sources, lose themselves in the river; over which a bridge is
built, that separates the sacred part from that which lies open to common

use. Vessels are allowed to come over this bridge, but no person is permitted to swim, except below it.

The Hispellates, to whom Augustus gave this place, furnish a public bath and likewise entertain all strangers, at their own expense. Several villas, attracted by the beauty of this river, are situated upon its borders. In short, every object that presents itself will afford you entertainment. You may also amuse yourself with numberless inscriptions, that are fixed upon the pillars and walls by different persons, celebrating the virtues of the fountain, and the divinity that presides over it. There are many of them you will greatly admire, as there are some that will make you laugh: but I must correct myself when I say so; you are too humane, I know, to laugh upon such an occasion. Farewell.

Pliny (trans. William Melmoth)

To Ailsa Rock

HEARKEN, thou craggy ocean pyramid!
   Give answer from thy voice, the sea-fowl's screams!
   When were thy shoulders mantled in huge streams?
When, from the sun, was thy broad forehead hid?
How long is 't since the mighty power bid
   Thee heave to airy sleep from fathom dreams?
   Sleep in the lap of thunder or sun-beams,
Or when grey clouds are thy cold cover-lid?
Thou answer'st not, for thou art dead asleep!
   Thy life is but two dead eternities—
The last in air, the former in the deep;
   First with the whales, last with the eagle-skies—
Drown'd wast thou till earthquake made thee steep,
   Another cannot wake thy giant size.

John Keats

ADVENTURE

Definition

IN TIME of peace in the modern world, if one is thoughtful and careful, it is rather more difficult to be killed or maimed in the outland places of the globe than it is in the streets of our great cities, but the atavistic urge toward danger persists and its satisfaction is called adventure. However, your adventurer feels no gratification in crossing Market Street in San Francisco against the traffic. Instead he will go to a good deal of trouble and expense to get himself killed in the South Seas. In reputedly rough water, he will go in a canoe; he will invade deserts without adequate food and he will expose his tolerant and uninoculated blood to strange viruses. This is adventure.

John Steinbeck and Edward F. Ricketts

The Rescue

WE SPREAD ourselves out in the form of a cross upon the snow, hoping that if we made a geometrical pattern we should attract the attention of the eyes which we knew must be watching from the ship. But our symbol of hope did not last very long, because its component parts broke away from one another, each occupied with his own particular activity. George tended the brazier set up once more upon the slope. He loaded it with moss and poured on to it the fuel oil, the last we had. At each dose of oil an evanescent puff of black smoke fled up the mountain-side and was gone. . . .

Suddenly I wanted to scream and smash something. I yelled and shouted at the top of my voice:

" Come on! Come on, she's coming in! Closer! Nearer! She's coming in, boys! Keep it up! Keep on waving! Wave like hell! She's coming. . . ."

But the evil spirit of the second point west of the observation camp had one more shot in his locker. As the whaler pulled away from the ship, a little speck from where we watched it vanishing and reappearing in the swell, the sky darkened over the western glacier. We saw the boat pull up-wind, the rhythmic strong sweep of her oars catching the light. From the glacier a dark veil of snow swept down upon her and ruffled the sea into a sudden anger. She disappeared. The dark veil spread on out to sea and hid the ship. We heard her blowing faintly.

" She's calling the boat back," we said.

Yet when the squall had passed on the whaler was still there pulling strongly for the shore, her bows turned towards us. Her oars moved as one with a sure and heartening beat.

Now we heaved the pram up from its bed of banked stones and suddenly our dwelling-place, our home, was no more. We had lain in shivering misery for what seemed an eternity under its shelter and now all at once it became just a damp hollow in a pile of stones, a place without meaning on an empty beach. And the roof of our house became again the bottom of a boat, blackened with soot from the brazier which still flickered half-way up the snow slope. We pulled the pram down to the sea and loaded into it our soiled and torn quadruple sleeping-bag, a few grimy chipped cups and plates, the primus stove, the enamel pail, two bent aluminium pannikins and the faithful saucepan. One of the pannikins held a little oatmeal, all the food we had left except the remains of the seal meat buried beneath the snow. That we bequeathed to the vultures. When the whaler stood off the reefs we pulled out to her.

But the old iron brazier still stands half-way up the snow slope at the second point west of the observation camp. We forgot to bring it away. It will never burn again. Higher still, above the moss platform where the terns will carry on their eternal business next summer, a tin of fuel oil stands beside a semi-circle of stones. The melting snow will bring the stones rattling down the slope next spring. The flag, dyed with penguins' blood, must have blown down long ago. And on the beach there lies a pair of sea-boots, my sea-boots, which Walker, the last to jump into the pram when we left, kicked off his feet on to the stones. If you ever go to the second point west of the observation camp and find them you may keep them. Pray that you never do.

F. D. Ommanney

Calonak Island

AFTER THIS isle men go by sea to another isle that is clept Calonak.

And in that isle there is a great marvel, more to speak of than in any other part of the world. For all manner of fishes, that be there in the sea about them, come once in the year—each manner of

148

d iverse fishes, one manner of kind after other. And they cast themselves to the sea bank of that isle so great plenty and multitude, that no man may anything see but fish. And there they abide three days. And every man of the country taketh of them as many as him liketh. And after, that manner of fish after the third day departeth and goeth into the sea.

And after them come another multitude of fish of another kind and do in the same manner as the first did, other three days. And after them another, till all the diverse manner of fishes have been there, and that men have taken of them that them liketh. And no man knoweth the cause wherefore it may be. But they of the country say that it is for to do reverence to their king, that is the most worthy king that is in the world as they say; because that he fulfilleth the commandment that God bade to Adam and Eve, when God said, *Crescite et multi-plicamini et replete terram*. And for because that he multiplieth so the world with children, therefore God sendeth him so the fishes of diverse kinds of all that be in the sea, to take at his will for him and all his people. And therefore all the fishes of the sea come to make him homage as the most noble and excellent king of the world, and that is best beloved with God, as they say. I know not the reason, why it is, but God knoweth; but this, me-seemeth, is the most marvel that ever I saw. For this marvel is against kind and not with kind, that the fishes that have freedom to environ all the coasts of the sea at their own list, come of their own will to proffer them to the death, without constraining of man. And therefore, I am siker that this may not be, without a great token.

There be also in that country a kind of snails that be so great, that many persons may lodge them in their shells, as men would do in a little house. And other snails there be that be full great but not so huge as the other. And of these snails, and of great white worms that have black heads that be as great as a man's thigh, and some less as great worms that men find there in woods, men make viand royal for the king and for other great lords. And if a man that is married die in that country, men bury his wife with him all quick; for men say there, that it is reason that she make him company in that other world as she did in this.

Sir John Mandeville

Octher's Voyage in the Year 890

OCTHER SAID that the country wherein he dwelt was called Helgo-
land. Octher told his lord King Alfred that he dwelt furthest north
of any other Norman. He said that he dwelt towards the north
part of the land towards the west coast, and affirmed that the land,
notwithstanding it stretcheth marvellous far towards the north, yet
it is all desert and not inhabited, unless it be very few places, here
and there, whence certain Finns dwell upon the coast, who live by
hunting all the winter, and by fishing in summer. He said that
upon a certain time he fell into a fantasy and desire to prove and know
how far that land stretched northward, and whether there were any
habitation of men north beyond the desert.

Whereupon he took his voyage directly north along the coast, having
upon his starboard always the desert land, and upon the leeboard the
main ocean, and continued his course for the space of three days. In
which space he was come as far towards the north, as commonly the
whale hunters use to travel. Whence he proceeded in his course still
towards the north so far as he was able to sail in other three days. At
the end whereof he perceived that the coast turned towards the east,
or else the sea opened with a main gulf into the land, he knew not how
far. Well he wist and remembered that he was fain to stay till he had
a western wind, and somewhat northerly: and thence he sailed plain
east along the coast still so far as he was able in the space of four days.
At the end of which time he was compelled again to stay till he had a
full northerly wind, forsomuch as the coast bowed thence directly
towards the south, or at least wise the sea opened into the land he could
not tell how far, so that he sailed thence along the coast continually
full south, so far as he could travel in five days; and at the fifth day's
end he discovered a mighty river which opened very far into the land.
At the entry of which river he stayed his course, and in conclusion
turned back again, for he durst not enter thereinto for fear of the
inhabitants of the land: perceiving that on the other side of the river
the country was thoroughly inhabited: which was the first peopled
land that he had found since his departure from his own dwelling:
whereas continually throughout all his voyage, he had evermore on his
starboard, a wilderness and desert country, except that in some places,
he saw a few fishers, fowlers, and hunters, which were all Finns: and

all the way upon his leeboard was the main ocean. The Biarmes had inhabited and tilled their country indifferent well, notwithstanding he was afraid to go upon shore. But the country of the Terfynnes lay all waste, and not inhabited, except as it were, as we have said, whereas dwelled certain hunters, fowlers, and fishers . . .

He said that the country of Norway was very long and small. So much of it as either beareth any good pasture, or may be tilled, lieth upon the sea coast, which notwithstanding in some places is very rocky and stony: and all eastward, all along against the inhabited land lie wild and huge hills and mountains, which are in some places inhabited by the Finns. The inhabited land is broadest toward the south and the further it stretcheth towards the north it groweth evermore smaller and smaller. Towards the south it is peradventure threescore miles in breadth or broader in some places: about the middest, thirty miles or above, and towards the north where it is smallest he affirmeth that it proveth not three miles from the sea to the mountains. The mountains be in breadth of such quantity as a man is able to travel over in a fortnight, and in some places no more than may be travelled in six days. Right over against this land in the other side of the mountains, somewhat towards the south, lieth Swethland, and against the same, towards the north, lieth Queeneland. The Queénes sometimes passing the mountains, invade and spoil the Normans; and on the contrary part, the Normans likewise sometimes spoil their country.

Richard Hakluyt

Pompey's Flight

WHEN POMPEY had got a little distance from the camp he quitted his horse. He had very few people about him; and, as he saw he was not pursued, he went softly on, wrapped up in such thoughts as we may suppose a man to have who had been used for thirty-four years to conquer and carry all before him, and now in his old age first came to know what it was to be defeated and to fly. We may easily conjecture what his thoughts must be when in one short hour he had lost the glory and the power which had been growing up amidst so many wars and conflicts; and he who was lately guarded with such armies of horse and foot, and such great and powerful fleets, was reduced to so mean and contemptible an equipage that his enemies, who were in search of him, could not know him.

He passed by Larissa and came to Tempe, where burning with

thirst he threw himself upon his face and drank out of the river, after which he passed through the valley and went down to the sea-coast. There he spent the remainder of the night in a poor fisherman's cabin. Next morning about break of day he went on board a small river-boat, taking with him such of his company as were freemen. The slaves he dismissed, bidding them go to Caesar and fear nothing.

As he was coasting along, he saw a ship of burden just ready to sail: the master of which was Peticius, a Roman citizen, who, though not acquainted with Pompey, knew him by sight. It happened that this man the night before dreamed he saw Pompey come and talk to him, not in the figure he had formerly known him, but in mean and melancholy circumstances. He was giving the passengers an account of his dream, as persons, who have a great deal of time upon their hands, love to discourse about such matters; when, on a sudden, one of the mariners told him he saw a little boat rowing up to him from the land, and the crew making signs, by shaking their garments and stretching out their hands. Upon this, Peticius stood up, and could distinguish Pompey among them in the same form as he had seen him in his dream. Then beating his head for sorrow, he ordered the seamen to let down the ship's boat, and held out his hand to Pompey to invite him aboard, for by his dress he perceived his change of fortune. Therefore, without waiting for any farther application, he took him up, and such of his companions as he thought proper, and then hoisted sail.

Plutarch (trans. Bernadotte Perrin)

On Safari

THE MOSQUITOES from which we sought protection are well known to every traveller in the tropics. I was reminded of Mark Twain's story of the time when they penetrated his netting in such numbers that at last he opened it, got them all inside, and then slept outside in comparative comfort.

But they are not the only trial of a safari. One night I heard a continuous scratching noise, and on turning on my torch found that I lay in the direct path of a party of Amazon ants. They were trekking through the tent and had already knocked several of my things to the ground. I knew it would be useless to engage them in battle and there was nothing to do but lie still and wait till they had passed. This took about two hours, after which I had some peace.

I had heard from the residents of the fierce hippo fly, " the only fly which can make a hippo sit up ". I did not seriously believe in this creature until one day near a pool I personally experienced what it could do. It came at me again and again whatever I did, though I did at last manage to frighten it off. Later on I saw a Portuguese official who had been bitten by a hippo fly and the resulting sore kept him prostrate for several days.

But in spite of these discomforts, a safari has immense charm. You are in a great free open country where you can wander at will. The sun may be intensely hot, but the early morning and the evening make up for it, and it is the joy of breaking camp at dawn which you remember afterwards, the streak of light in the sky, then the sudden day. There are surprises at every turn in the path where every beast and bird and flower is new, and when evening comes and the boys sit round their fire it is pleasant to hear their cheerful voices and their weird songs and instruments. At night the moonlight is so brilliant that you can read by it, and if the sudden roar of a lion breaks the silence, it is only an added thrill. The mere thought of that splendid note makes me long for the wild again.

W. Lavallin Puxley

A Traveller's Tale

> . . . I SPAKE of most disastrous chances,
> Of moving accidents by flood and field,
> Of hair-breadth 'scapes i' the imminent deadly breach,
> Of being taken by the insolent foe
> And sold to slavery, of my redemption thence
> And portance in my travel's history;
> Wherein of antres vast and deserts idle,
> Rough quarries, rocks and hills whose heads touch heaven,
> It was my hint to speak, such was the process;
> And of the Cannibals that each other eat,
> The Anthropophagi, and men whose heads
> Do grow beneath their shoulders. . . .

William Shakespeare

A Plan for Australian Exploration, 1715

THENCE TAKE my departur and stear west till I come to the Solomon Islands, which are reported by the Spaniards to abound in Gold; They were discovered above 100 years agoe, but the Court of Spain did not thinck fit to settle them, by reason they had not intirely setled the main land of Peru.

These Islands lying out of the way of all foreign Trade, and the Accapulca Ships which trade betweene the Philippine Islands in the East Indies and Accapulca on the Coast of Mexico in the South Seas, keepe always in the North East Trade wind, when they sail from Accapulca to the Philippines, and when they come from the Indies to Accapulca . . . as soon as I come to theese Islands, I propose to goe a Shore with about 150 men to search and discover what the Country abounds in, and then trapan some of the Inhabitants on board, and bring them for England, who when they have learned our language, will be proper interpreters.

From the Solomon Islands I propose to sail west, to the Coast of Nova Guinea, which is the East Side of Nova Hollandia, in the East Indies, and make a true discovery of that Coast, and search what the Country abounds in: it lying North and South as Peru does, and in the same Lat^d I believe it abounds in Gold and Silver mines, which if discovered and setled may be of vast advantage to Great Britain. This Coast is full of Harbours, according to the Account I have had out of Spanish Journals of the discovery of the Solomon Islands. After I have made a discovery of this Coast of Nova Guinea, and taken away some of the Inhabitants, I propose to make a farther discovery of Nova Britannia and the adjacent Islands, and search what they abound in, and take off some of the Inhabitants likewise. For tho Capt Dampire discovered Nova Britannia yet he never was at Shore at any place, except Port Montegue, and only as far as the watering place, he having only 50 men in his Ship, was not strong enough to search the Country, and consequently it is unknowne what those parts abound in.

From Nova Britannia I propose to Sail to the westward, and sail between the west end of Nova Guinea and the Island of Gillolo, and stand away to the South ward of the Island of Java, and stear directly towards the Cape de bon Espirance . . . from thence sail for England.

John Welbe

Madeira

WE SAILED to the islands of Portum Sanctum, and then to Madeira, in which were sundry countries and islands, as Eractelenty, Magnefortis, Grancanary, Teneriffe, Palme Ferro, etc. And our captain went with his soldiers to land. And at our first coming near unto the river in one of these islands, as we refreshed ourselves among the date trees, in the land of the palms, by the sweet wells, we did, to the great fear of us all, see a great battle between the dragon and the unicorn; and, as God would, the unicorn thrust the dragon to the heart; and, again, the dragon with his tail stung the unicorn to death. Here is a piece of his horn; the blood of dragons is rich; that battle was worth two hundred marks to our captain.

Then we travelled further into Teneriffe, into an exceeding high mountain, above the middle region, whereas we had great plenty of rock alum, and might well hear an heavenly harmony among the stars. The moon was near hand us with marvellous heat; and when we came down at the hill-foot grew many gross herbs, as lovage, laserpitium, acanthus and solanum: whether it was by the eating of solanum or no, there was a great mighty man naked and hairy, in a deep sleep, whom we gently suffered to lie still. He had a great beard in which a bird did breed, and brought her young ones meat; this man slept half a year and waked not. . . .

In the isle called Ruc, in the great Can's land, I did see mermaids and satyrs with other fishes by night came four miles from the sea, and climbed into trees, and did eat dates and nutmegs, with whom the apes and baboons had much fighting, yelling and crying. The people of that land do live by eating the flesh of women. In this land did I see an ape play at tick-tack and after at Irish on the tables with one of that land; and also a parrot give one of their gentlewomen a checkmate at chess.

William Bullein

Kitten Overboard

A MOST TRAGICAL Incident fell out this day at Sea. While the Ship was under Sail, but making, as will appear, no great Way, a Kitten, one of four of the Feline Inhabitants of the Cabin, fell from the Window into the Water: an Alarm was immediately given to the Captain, who was then upon Deck, and received it with the utmost Concern and many bitter oaths. He immediately gave Orders to the Steersman in favour of the poor Thing, as he called it; the Sails were instantly slackened, and all Hands, as the Phrase is, employed to recover the poor Animal. I was, I own, extremely surprised at all this; less, indeed, at the Captain's extreme Tenderness, than at his conceiving any Possibility of Success; for, if Puss had had nine thousand, instead of nine Lives, I concluded they had been all lost.

The Boatswain, however, had more sanguine Hopes; for, having stript himself of his Jacket, Breeches, and Shirt, he leapt boldly into the Water, and, to my great Astonishment, in a few Minutes, returned to the Ship, bearing the motionless Animal in his Mouth. Nor was this, I observed, a Matter of such great Difficulty as it appeared to my Ignorance, and possibly may seem to that of my Freshwater Reader. The Kitten was now exposed to Air and Sun on the Deck, where its Life, of which it retained no Symptoms, was despaired of by all.

The Captain's humanity, if I may so call it, did not so totally destroy his Philosophy, as to make him yield himself up to affliction on this melancholy Occasion. Having felt his Loss like a Man, he resolved to shew he could bear it like one; and, having declared he had rather have lost a Cask of Rum or Brandy, betook himself to threshing at Backgammon with the Portuguese Friar, in which innocent Amusement they passed about two-thirds of their Time.

But as I have, perhaps, a little too wantonly endeavoured to raise the tender Passions of my Readers, in this Narrative, I should think myself unpardonable if I concluded it without giving them the Satisfaction of hearing that the Kitten at last recovered, to the great Joy of the good Captain. . . .

Henry Fielding

LANDFALL

WE PUSH on rapidly, lest the news of our coming might reach the people of Bunder Ujiji before we come in sight, and are ready for them. We halt at a little brook, then ascend the long slope of a naked ridge, the very last of the myriads we have crossed. This alone prevents us from seeing the lake in all its vastness. We arrive at the summit, travel across and arrive at its western rim, and— pause, reader—the port of Ujiji is below us, embowered in the palms, only five hundred yards from us! At this grand moment we do not think of the hundreds of miles we have marched, of the hundreds of hills that we have ascended and descended, of the many forests we have traversed, of the jungles and thickets that annoyed us, of the fervid salt plains that blistered our feet, of the hot suns that scorched us, nor the dangers and difficulties, now happily surmounted. At last the sublime hour has arrived!—our dreams, our hopes, and antici- pations are now about to be realized! Our hearts and our feelings are with our eyes, as we peer into the palms and try to make out in which hut or house lives the white man with the grey beard we heard about on the Malagarazi . . .

We were now about three hundred yards from the village of Ujiji, and the crowds are dense about me . . .

In the meantime, the head of the Expedition had halted, and the *kirangozi* was out of the ranks, holding his flag aloft, and Selim said to me, " I see the Doctor, sir. Oh, what an old man! He has got a white beard." And I—what would I not have given for a bit of friendly wilderness, where, unseen, I might vent my joy in some mad freak, such as idiotically biting my hand, turning a somersault, or slashing at trees, in order to allay those exciting feelings that were well-nigh uncontrollable. My heart beats fast, but I must not let my face betray my emotions, lest it shall detract from the dignity of a white man appearing under such extraordinary circumstances.

So I did that which I thought was most dignified. I pushed back the crowds, and, passing from the rear, walked down a living avenue of people, until I came in front of the semicircle of Arabs in front of which stood the white man with the grey beard. As I advanced slowly towards him I noticed he was pale, looked wearied, had a grey beard, wore a bluish cap with a faded gold band round it, had on a red-sleeved waistcoat, and a pair of grey tweed trousers. I would have run to him, only I was a coward in the presence of such a mob—would have embraced him, only, he being an Englishman, I did not know how he would receive me; so I did what cowardice and false pride suggested was the best thing—walked deliberately to him, took off my hat, and said:

" Dr. Livingstone, I presume? "

" YES," said he, with a kind smile, lifting his cap slightly.

Henry M. Stanley

I Never Saw that Land Before

I NEVER saw that land before,
And now can never see it again;
Yet, as if by acquaintance hoar
Endeared, by gladness and by pain,
Great was the affection that I bore

To the valley and the river small,
The cattle, the grass, the bare ash trees,
The chickens from the farmsteads, all
Elm-hidden, and the tributaries
Descending at equal intervals;

The blackthorns down along the brook
With wounds yellow as crocuses
Where yesterday the labourer's hook
Had sliced them cleanly; and the breeze
That hinted all and nothing spoke.

I neither expected anything
Nor yet remembered: but some goal
I touched then; and if I could sing
What would not even whisper my soul
As I went on my journeying,

I should use, as the trees and birds did,
A language not to be betrayed;
And what was hid should still be hid
Excepting from those like he made
Who answer when such whispers bid.

Edward Thomas

Columbus Discovers the New World

I

THEY CONTINUED their course until two in the morning, when a gun from the *Pinta* gave the joyful signal of land.

The land was now clearly seen about two leagues distant, where-upon they took in sail, and laid to, waiting impatiently for the dawn. The thoughts and feelings of Columbus in this little space of time must have been tumultuous and intense. At length, in spite of every difficulty and danger, he had accomplished his object. The great mystery of the ocean was revealed; his theory, which had been the scoff of sages, was triumphantly established; he had secured to himself a glory which must be as durable as the world itself.

It is difficult even for the imagination to conceive the feelings of such a man at the moment of so sublime a discovery. What a bewildering crowd of conjectures must have thronged upon his mind, as to the land which lay before him, covered with darkness! That it was fruitful was evident from the vegetables which floated from its shores. He thought, too, that he perceived in the balmy air the fragrance of aromatic groves. The moving light which he had beheld, had proved that it was the residence of man. But what were its inhabitants? Were they like those of the other parts of the globe; or were they some strange and monstrous race, such as the imagination in those times was prone to give to all remote and unknown regions? Had he come upon some wild island far in the Indian Sea; or was this the famed Cipango itself, the object of his golden fancies? A thousand speculations of the kind must have swarmed upon him, as, with his anxious crews, he waited for the night to pass away, wondering whether the morning light would reveal a savage wilderness, or dawn upon spicy groves, and glittering fanes, and gilded cities, and all the splendour of oriental civilization.

Washington Irving

II

THERE WAS an Indian, who had known no change,
    Who strayed content along a sunlit beach
Gathering shells. He heard a sudden strange
    Commingled noise; looked up; and gasped for speech,
For in the bay, where nothing was before,
    Moved on the sea, by magic, huge canoes,

With bellying clothes on poles, and not one oar,
  And fluttering coloured signs and clambering crews.

And he, in fear, this naked man alone,
  His fallen hands forgetting all their shells,
His lips gone pale, knelt low behind a stone,
  And stared, and saw, and did not understand,
Columbus's doom-burdened caravels
Slant to the shore, and all their seamen land.

Sir John Squire

Facing West

FACING west from California's shores,
Inquiring, tireless, seeking what is yet unfound,
I, a child, very old, over waves, towards the house of maternity, the
  land of migrations, look afar,
Look off the shores of my Western sea, the circle almost circled;
For starting westward from Hindustan, from the vales of Kashmere,
From Asia, from the north, from the God, the sage, and the hero,
From the south, from the flowery peninsulas and the spice islands,
Long having wander'd since, round the earth having wander'd,
Now I face home again, very pleas'd and joyous,
(But where is what I started for so long ago?
And why is it yet unfound?)

Walt Whitman

Homeward Bound

THE TRAVELLER was homeward bound, and his liner made its land-
fall, and turned for Portland and its London pilot. There was no
welcome in that look of the coast of home. The shadow of land to
port might have been the end of all the headlands of the seas. It
was as desolate as antiquity by twilight. There was no rain, but
the chill cut to the bone. The sky was old and dark. This frown
of the North-land subdued the comfortable life of the ship; it fled
below. The little cheerful groups dissolved without a word. The
decks were deserted except for two odd figures, muffled like mum-
mies in a shelter on the lee side. He could find nobody who would
face it with him. He strolled aft to the shelter where some men who
knew the East used to meet, before dinner, to smoke and yarn, but

only a steward was there, a disillusioned familiar who was brusquely piling the unwanted wicker chairs—throwing them at each other.

Somehow even the satin-wood panelling of the stairway to the saloon, with its bronze balustrade, appeared now to be out of place. It did not accord with cold draughts. The glow-lamps shone in emptiness, the palms in the corners were dingy. He suspected the life of the ship had suddenly absented itself, and was behind closed doors, whispering of a crisis to which he could get no clue. As he descended to his cabin he paused to watch an officer, muffled in a great-coat, pass from one side of the ship to the other on a deck above him, but the man was preoccupied and hurried, and did not notice that the ship had another lonely ghost wandering about her.

In his cabin the little gilt image of a Buddha, Putai Ho-shang, the god of children and earthly joys, passive and happy, regarded him cheerfully from the clothes chest. That token of the East had more sun in it than all the world into which the steamer had now come. The image was old, perhaps as old as that fading recollection of a land along which the ship was now cruising for haven. Might not that recollection fade utterly before the haven was reached? Was that image cheerful with tidings that were nearer to the springs of life than anything known under the skies of the North? Was it that knowledge which made it confident? There was a suggestion of derision about its happy smile, as though it had a word which made it invulnerable to this bleak air, and to the driving darkness that was the headlong confusion of a region which had lost its light and faith.

The bugle called to dinner. He took no notice of it. He thought he would sooner pack up; at least he could then confirm, putting away some good things he had found in Brunei, Palembang, and Pekin, that somewhere life was ardent and young, and was light-hearted while making beautiful things. He placed a porcelain bowl beside the Buddha. The two were worth looking at. If you stood in a certain way a golden dragon was hinted in the azure of the bowl. The man who made that did not work in a north-east wind. When he opened his camphor-wood chest it filled his cabin with a suggestion of warm nights, of a still sea in which the reflection of the stars were comets rising from the deeps, of the figures of motionless palms drowsing with their heads above a beach. Well, that was over. But he had seen it. Time, now, to put it away, except as a private thought.

H. M. Tomlinson

Ye Who Have Toiled

YE WHO have toil'd uphill to reach the haunt
Of other men who lived in other days,
Whether the ruins of a citadel
Raised on the summit by Pelasgic hands,
Or chamber of the distaff and the song.
Ye will not tell what treasures there ye found,
But I will.
    Ye found there the viper laid
Full-length, flat-headed, on a sunny slab,
Nor loth to hiss at ye while crawling down.
Ye saw the owl flap the loose ivy-leaves
And, hooting, shake the berries on your heads.
    Now, was it worth your while to mount so high
Merely to say you did it, and to ask
If those about you ever did the like?
Believe me, O my friends, 'twere better far
To stretch your limbs along the level sand
As they do, where small children scoop the drift,
Thinking it must be gold, where curlews soar
And scales drop glistening from the prey above . . .

Walter Savage Landor

Soul of Canada

THE RIDE is over, but these are my possessions. Wherever I go from
here these will go with me.

Always for me there will be mountains running down to the
Pacific, great trees and tiny trails and deer, and packers lighting fires
and pitching tents and hauling up the slack on a diamond hitch; there
will be year-old snow and black tea out of billycans and rain in the
mountains; but no rain on the scorching range of the dry belt,
only cactus and sage-brush and sunflowers burning down the
hillsides.

Rain and sun in the foothills though, rivers and ranches, great
fantastic western saddles on little lean broncos, steers bucking at
stampedes, ten-gallon hats and high-heeled boots and close-fitting

overalls on bandy legs, horses milling in high corrals and little ranch-houses filling with unexpected guests. After that, sunset over the wheatfields and northern lights arching up the sky, and straight sandy roads which go on almost for ever, and elevators and cottonwood trees and the rare delight of river valleys.

Then Winnipeg and the wilderness beyond, and tameracks burning gold out of the blue swamps, naked rocks and lonely lakes shivering in the wind. Then the vast expanse of Lake Superior, and so winter on the farm—lamplight in the early morning kitchen—milking time in misty barns—teams labouring out of the bush—spring and syrup-boiling under budding maples, daisied hay standing high, and a boat floating down a river on the trail of a timber drive.

Autumn again under the shoulder of the Laurentians, and so at last this gold and silver journey through the Green Mountains of Vermont. And always through everything the horses with me, tireless and kind, giving me their unbroken trust. Remembering Canada, I remember, too, the majesty of Vancouver, standing between the mountains and the sea, Calgary and Winnipeg on the borders of the Prairies, Ottawa with the Parliament Houses standing upon their hill, and Montreal grouped round its royal mountain.

But when seas divide me from her, Canada will live for me, not in the memory of her cities, but of hip-roofed barns and snake fences and stout corrals, of the dark flash of a red-winged blackbird and the snort of a little branded bronco, of mountains and wheatfields and the wilderness. The soul of Canada is not in her cities.

For the soul of the world has fled from cities. And if it is ever to inhabit them again it is from mountains and wheatfields and the sea that it must return.

Mary Bosanquet

Home-Thoughts From Abroad

OH, TO be in England
Now that April's there,
And whoever wakes in England
Sees, some morning, unaware,
That the lowest boughs and the brushwood sheaf
Round the elm-tree bole are in tiny leaf,
While the chaffinch sings on the orchard bough
In England—now!

And after April, when May follows,
And the whitethroat builds, and all the swallows!
Hark, where my blossomed pear-tree in the hedge
Leans to the field and scatters on the clover
Blossoms and dewdrops—at the bent spray's edge—
That's the wise thrush; he sings each song twice over,
Lest you should think he never could recapture
The first fine careless rapture!
And though the fields look rough with hoary dew,
All will be gay when noontide wakes anew
The buttercups, the little children's dower
—Far brighter than this gaudy melon-flower!

Robert Browning

The First Landing in Virginia

THE SECOND of July we found shoal water, which smelt so sweetly, and was so strong a smell, as if we had been in the midst of some delicate garden, abounding with all kinds of odoriferous flowers; by which we were assured that the land could not be far distant. And keeping good watch and bearing but slack sail, the fourth of the same month we arrived upon the coast, which we supposed to be a continent and firm land, and we sailed along the same 120 English miles before we could find any entrance, or river issuing into the Sea. The first that appeared unto us we entered, though not without some difficulty, and cast anchor about three arquebus-shot within the haven's mouth, on the left hand of the same; and after thanks given to God for our safe arrival thither, we manned our boats, and went to view the land next adjoining, and to take possession of the same in the right of the Queen's most excellent Majesty, as rightful Queen and Princess of the same, and after delivered the same over to your use, according to the ceremonies used in such enterprises, we viewed the land about us, being, whereas we first landed, very sandy and low towards the water side, but so full of grapes as the very beating and surge of the sea overflowed them. Of which we found such plenty, as well there as in all places else, both on the sand and on the green soil on the hills, as in the plains, as well on every little shrub, as also climbing towards the tops of high Cedars, that I think in all the world the like abundance is not to be found: and myself

166

having seen those parts of Europe that most abound, find such difference as were incredible to be written.

We passed from the sea side towards the tops of those hills next adjoining, being but of mean height; and from thence we beheld the Sea on both sides, to the North and to the South, finding no end any of both ways. This land lay stretching itself to the West, which after we found to be but an Island of twenty leagues long, and not above six miles broad. Under the bank or hill whereon we stood, we beheld the valleys replenished with goodly Cedar trees, and having discharged our arquebus-shot, such a flock of Cranes (the most part white) arose under us, with such a cry redoubled by many Echoes, as if an army of men had shouted all together . . .

We remained by the side of this Island two whole days before we saw any people of the Country. The third day we espied one small boat rowing towards us, having in it three persons. This boat came to the land's side, four arquebus-shot from our ships; and there two of the people remaining, the third came along the shore side towards us, and we being then all within board, he walked up and down upon the point of the land next unto us. Then the Master and the Pilot of the Admiral, Simon Ferdinando, and the Captain, Philip Amadas, myself, and others, rowed to the land; whose coming this fellow attended, never making any show of fear or doubt. And after he had spoken of many things not understood by us, we brought him, with his own good liking, aboard the ships, and gave him a shirt, a hat, and some other things, and made him taste of our wine and our meat, which he liked very well; and, after having viewed both barks, he departed, and went to his own boat again, which he had left in a little cove or creek adjoining. As soon as he was two bow-shot into the water he fell to fishing, and in less than half an hour he had laden his boat as deep as it could swim, with which he came again to the point of the land, and there he divided his fish into two parts, pointing one part to the ship and the other to the pinnace. Which, after he had as much as he might requited the former benefits received, departed out of our sight.

Richard Hakluyt

You Will Remember

YOU WILL remember, lady, how the morn
Came slow above the Isle of Athelney,
And all the flat lands lying to the sky
Were shrouded sea-like in a veil of grey,
As, standing on a little rounded hill,
We placed our hands upon the Holy Thorn.

Do you remember in what hopeful fear
We gazed behind us, thinking we might see
Arthur come striding through the high, bright corn,
Or Alfred resting on a Saxon spear?
And as the cold mists melted from the fields
We seemed to hear the winding of a horn.

You will remember how we walked the Vale
Through Meare and Westhay unto Godney End;
And how we said: " Time is an endless lane
And Life a little mile without a bend. . . .
Behind us what? Before us, if we ran,
Might we not be in time to see the Grail? "

H. V. Morton

Harlech Bay

WE CAST anchor in the very midmost of that solemn bay with its half-circle of huge mountains looking down upon an empty sea. The giants were dim in the haze, but the more enormous, and I revered and worshipped them.

We so cast anchor because I had to wait for the tide. I could not run up the long, winding channel through the sands of Port Madoc until the flood should be with me, and that would not be till the gloaming, between eight and nine o'clock that night.

Therefore did we lie thus in Harlech Bay, gazing at the great hills of Wales. There is no corner of Europe that I know, not even the splendid amphitheatre standing in tiers of high Alpine wall around Udine, which so moves me with awe and majesty of great things as does this mass of the northern Welsh mountains seen from this corner of their silent sea.

Few can recall it, for few visit that corner of the salt. It leads nowhere but to the harbour of Port Madoc. No man beaches a boat today under Harlech; no man today sets out from that shore for Ireland beyond. The halls are in ruin. There is no more harping. No flight of sails comes up eastward out of the sea like birds. Even the sailors have forgotten Gwynnedd. Today the only sailors familiar with the solemnity of which I speak are those who ply in the small boats of the Slate Trade, or who, like myself, have employed a curious leisure in searching out new things here in the seas of home. For all my life I have made discoveries close at hand, and have found the Island of Britain to be infinite. But who in our time knows where to look for vision?

Indeed, this lack of fame applies to perhaps half the greater visions, even of the modern over-frequented and travelled earth. Men know half of them to satiety, but the other half they never see. Every one has wearied of the Bay of Naples, repeated a thousand times, but what of that lonely field by the flat Adriatic sand whence you may see the dark eastern Fall of the Gran Sasso, tragic, with storms about it, dominating a deserted shore? Everybody has his bellyful of Gavarnie, but what of the valley of Araxas, which proclaims so terribly the glory of God? Where are the pictures of that? Who has drawn it? Yet it is but half a day from Gavarnie.

So it is with this awful parade of great mountains standing on guard over the northern corner of Cardigan Bay, seen from the silence and the flat of ocean, towering above its glass; and all that late afternoon and evening I adored them until, with the last of the light, and a westerly air which was but the suggestion of a breeze, we groped north anxiously for the opening to Port Madoc channel.

Hilaire Belloc

Outpost

SEVEN WEEKS of sea, and twice seven days of storm
Upon the huge Atlantic, and once more
We ride into still water and the calm
Of a sweet evening, screened by either shore
Of Spain and Barbary. Our toils are o'er,
Our exile is accomplished. Once again

We look on Europe, mistress as of yore
Of the fair earth and of the hearts of men.
Ay, this is the famed rock which Hercules
And Goth and Moor bequeathed us. At this door
England stands sentry. God! to hear the shrill
Sweet treble of her fifes upon the breeze,
And at the summons of the rock gun's roar
To see her red coats marching from the hill!

Wilfrid Scawen Blunt

Mungo Park Discovers the Niger

JULY 20th. In the morning I endeavoured, both by entreaties, and threats, to procure some victuals from the Dooty, but in vain. I even begged some corn from one of his female slaves, as she was washing it at the well, and had the mortification to be refused. However, when the Dooty was gone to the fields, his wife sent me a handful of meal, which I mixed with water, and drank for breakfast. About eight o'clock, I departed from Doolinkeaboo, and at noon stopped a few minutes at a large *Korree*; where I had some milk given me by the Foulahs. And hearing that two Negroes were going from thence to Sego, I was happy to have their company, and we set out immediately. About four o'clock we stopped at a small village, where one of the Negroes met with an acquaintance, who invited us to a sort of public entertainment, which was conducted with more than common propriety. A dish made of sour milk and meal, called *Sinkatoo*, and beer made from their corn, was distributed with great liberality; and the women were admitted into the society: a circumstance I had never before observed in Africa. There was no compulsion; every one was at liberty to drink as he pleased: they nodded to each other when about to drink, and on setting down the calabash, commonly said *berka* (thank you). Both men and women appeared to be somewhat intoxicated, but they were far from being quarrelsome.

Departing from thence, we passed several large villages where I was constantly taken for a Moor, and became the subject of much merriment to the Bambarrans; who, seeing me drive my horse before me, laughed heartily at my appearance.—He has been at Mecca, says one; you may see that by his clothes: another asked if my horse was sick; a third wished to purchase it, etc.; so that I believe the very slaves were ashamed to be seen in my company. Just before it was dark, we took up our lodging for the night at a small village, where I procured some victuals for myself and some corn for my horse, at the moderate price of a button; and was told that I should see the Niger (which the Negroes call Joliba or *the great water*), early the next day. The lions are here very numerous: the gates are shut a little after sunset, and nobody allowed to go out. The thoughts of seeing the Niger in the morning, and the troublesome buzzing of musketoes, prevented me from shutting my eyes during the night; and I had saddled my horse, and was in readiness before daylight; but, on account of the wild beasts, we were obliged to wait until the people were stirring, and the gates opened. This happened to be market day at Sego, and the roads were everywhere filled with people carrying different articles to sell. We passed four large villages, and at eight o'clock saw the smoke over Sego.

As we approached the town, I was fortunate enough to overtake the fugitive Kaartans, to whose kindness I had been so much indebted in my journey through Bambarra. They readily agreed to introduce me to the king; and we rode together through some marshy ground, where, as I was anxiously looking around for the river, one of them called out *geo affilli* (see the water); and looking forwards, I saw with infinite pleasure the great object of my mission; the long sought for majestic Niger, glittering to the morning sun, as broad as the Thames at Westminster, and flowing slowly *to the eastward*. I hastened to the brink, and, having drank of the water, lifted up my fervent thanks in prayer, to the Great Ruler of all things, for having thus far crowned my endeavours with success.

Mungo Park

Arrival

TRAVELLING by the ordinary routes, you meet the American people a week before you meet America. And my excitement to discover what, precisely, this nation was *at*, was inflamed rather than damped by the attitude of a charming American youth who crossed by the same boat. That simplicity that is not far down in any American was very beautifully on the delightful surface with him. The second day out he sidled shyly up to me. " Of what nationality *are* you? " he asked. His face showed bewilderment when he heard. " I thought all Englishmen had moustaches," he said. I told him of the infinite variety, within the homogeneity, of our race. He did not listen, but settled down near me with the eager kindliness of a child. "You know," he said, "you'll never understand America. No, sir. No Englishman can understand America. I've been in London. In your Houses of Parliament there is one door for peers to go in at, and one for ordinary people. Did I laugh some when I saw that? You bet your, America's not like that. In America one man's just as good as another. You'll never understand America." I was all humility. His theme and his friendliness fired him. He rose with a splendour which, I had to confess to myself, England could never have given to him. "Would you like to hear me re-cite to you the Declaration of Independence?" he asked. And he did.

Rupert Brooke

The First Sight of Mexico

THEY HAD not advanced far, when, turning an angle of the sierra, they suddenly came on a view which more than compensated the toils of the preceding day. It was that of the valley of Mexico, or Tenochtitlan, as more commonly called by the natives; which, with its picturesque assemblage of water, woodland, and cultivated plains, its shining cities and shadowy hills, was spread out like some gay and gorgeous panorama before them. In the highly rarefied atmosphere of these upper regions, even remote objects have a brilliancy of colouring and a distinctness of outline which seem to annihilate distance. Stretching far away at their feet were seen noble forests of oak, sycamore, and cedar, and beyond, yellow fields of maize and the towering maguey, intermingled with orchards and blooming gardens; for flowers, in such demand for their religious festivals, were even more abundant in this populous valley than in other parts of Anahuac. In the centre of the great basin were beheld the lakes, occupying then a much larger portion of its surface than at present; their borders thickly studded with towns and hamlets, and, in the midst—like some Indian empress with her coronal of pearls—the fair city of Mexico, with her white towers and pyramidal temples, reposing, as it were, on the bosom of the waters—the far-famed " Venice of the Aztecs ". High over all rose the royal hill of Chapoltepec, the residence of the Mexican monarchs, crowned with the same grove of gigantic cypresses which at this day fling their broad shadows over the land.

In the distance beyond the blue waters of the lake, and nearly screened by intervening foliage, was seen a shining speck, the river capital of Tezcuco, and, still further on, the dark belt of porphyry, girdling the valley around like a rich setting which Nature had devised for the fairest of her jewels. . . .

What, then, must have been the emotions of the Spaniards, when, after working their toilsome way into the upper air, the cloudy tabernacle parted before their eyes, and they beheld these fair scenes in all their pristine magnificence and beauty! It was like the spectacle which greeted the eyes of Moses from the summit of Pisgah; and, in the warm glow of their feelings, they cried out, " It is the promised land! "

William H. Prescott

Prospice

FEAR DEATH?—to feel the fog in my throat,
    The mist in my face,
When the snows begin, and the blasts denote
    I am nearing the place,
The power of the night, the press of the storm,
    The post of the foe;
Where he stands, the Arch Fear in a visible form,
    Yet the strong man must go:
For the journey is done and the summit attained,
    And the barriers fall,
Though a battle's to fight ere the guerdon be gained,
    The reward of it all.
I was ever a fighter, so—one fight more,
    The best and the last!
I would hate that death bandaged my eyes, and forbore,
    And bade me creep past.
No! let me taste the whole of it, fare like my peers
    The heroes of old,
Bear the brunt, in a minute pay glad life's arrears
    Of pain, darkness and cold.
For sudden the worst turns the best to the brave,
    The black minute's at end,
And the elements' rage, the fiend-voices that rave,
    Shall dwindle, shall blend,

173

Shall change, shall become first a peace out of pain,
   Then a light, then thy breast,
O thou soul of my soul! I shall clasp thee again,
   And with God be the rest!

Robert Browning

INDEX OF AUTHORS

INDEX OF SOURCES

51 THE SUSSEX DOWNS. Gilbert White, *Natural History of Selborne*.
O THE SWEET VALLEY. William Morris, from "The Life and Death of Jason".

52 A VALE IN IDA. Lord Tennyson, from "Oenone".
KU-LING PASS. Captain William Gill, *The River of Golden Sand*.

53 SPRING. James Thomson, from "The Seasons".

54 THE MOUNTAIN ROAD. R. L. Stevenson, *Travels with a Donkey*.

55 NOCTURNE. Lord Tennyson.
SOUTHERN ITALY. John Ruskin, *Modern Painters*; reprinted by permission of Messrs. George Allen & Unwin Ltd.

56 THE SUBLIME. Wilfrid Scawen Blunt; reprinted by permission of the trustees of the author's estate, and of Messrs. Secker & Warburg Ltd.
THE ALPS. Sir Leslie Stephen, *The Playground of Europe*; reprinted by permission of Messrs. Longmans, Green, & Co., Ltd.

57 THE RAVINE. Percy Bysshe Shelley, from "Mont Blanc".

58 NIAGARA FALLS. Rupert Brooke, *Letters from America*; reprinted by permission of the author's representatives, and of Messrs. Sidgwick & Jackson Ltd.

59 TO HIS TUTOR. John Hall.

63 THE TRUE TRAVELLER. W. H. Mallock, *In An Enchanted Isle*; reprinted by permission of Messrs. Curtis Brown Ltd.
STEPPING WESTWARD. William Wordsworth.

64 STRANGE CITIES. James Pope-Hennessy, *America is an Atmosphere*; reprinted by permission of the author, and of Messrs. Home & Van Thal Ltd.

65 NINTH-CENTURY INDIA. Renaudat's translation (1733) of *Travels of Two Mahomedans in India and China in the Ninth Century*.

66 THE WANDERER. Percy Bysshe Shelley.

67 TEIRESIAS ADVISES ODYSSEUS. Homer, *The Odyssey*, Book XI, translated by E. V. Rieu; reprinted by permission of the translator, and of Penguin Books Ltd.

68 O'ER DESERT PLAINS. William Shenstone.

69 WANDERER IN WIMBLEDON. E. M. Forster, *Howards End*; reprinted by permission of Messrs. Edward Arnold & Company.

71 RESOLUTION AND INDEPENDENCE. William Wordsworth.
THE WINTER SUN. Jeremy Taylor, from a sermon "The Duties of the Tongue".

72 YOUNG TRAVELLERS. William Cowper, from "The Progress of Error".

73 THE STAGE COACH. Washington Irving, *The Sketch Book*.

74 ENCHANTED GROUND. Charles Dickens, *The Uncommercial Traveller*.

75 THE LISTENERS. Walter de la Mare; reprinted by permission of the poet, and of Messrs. Faber & Faber Ltd.

76 CAMP FOR THE NIGHT. Marjorie Kinnan Rawlings, *Cross Creek*; reprinted by permission of the author, and of the author's agent.

77 OVER THE TIMOR SEA. Charles H. Holmes, *A Passport Round the World*; reprinted by permission of the author, and of Messrs. Hutchinson & Co., (Publishers) Ltd.

78 LETTER FROM TURKEY. Lady Mary Wortley Montagu, from a letter to the Countess of Mar, 1717.

79 THE FACE OF THE DESERT. Rudyard Kipling, *Letters of Travel*; reprinted by permission of Mrs. George Bambridge, and of Messrs. Macmillan & Co., Ltd.

80 WINTER IN THE ANTARCTIC. Sir Ernest Shackleton, *South*; reprinted by permission of Messrs. William Heinemann Ltd.

81 THE NILE. Leigh Hunt.
LURE OF RIVERS. H. D. Thoreau, *A Week on the Concord*.

85 TRAVELLERS. Laurence Sterne, *A Sentimental Journey*.

86 PARISIANS. E. Œ. Somerville and Martin Ross, *Stray-Aways*; reprinted by permission of Dr. Somerville, and of Messrs. Longmans, Green, & Co., Ltd.

87 AN ITALIAN IN AMERICA, 1524. John Verrazzano, *The Principal Navigations, etc., of the English Nation*, edited by Richard Hakluyt.
A BRITON IN HOLLAND. Oliver Goldsmith, from a letter to the Rev. Thomas Contarine, from Leyden, May 6, 1754.

89 THE ENGLISH. William Shakespeare, *King Henry the Fifth*, Act III, Scene VII.
LONDON, 1827. Heinrich Heine, *English Fragments*, (translated in the Camelot Series) edited by Havelock Ellis and Ernest Rhys; reprinted by permission of Messrs. J. M. Dent & Sons Ltd.

91 AT BOSSEKOP. Olive Murray Chapman, *Across Lapland*; reprinted by permission of Messrs. John Lane The Bodley Head Ltd.

92 THE AFRICAN NUBAS. J. A. Spender, *Men and Things*; reprinted by permission of Messrs. Cassell & Company, Ltd.

93 OLD MAN OF THE SEA. John Steinbeck and Edward F. Ricketts, *Sea of Cortez*; reprinted by permission of the authors, and of the Viking Press, New York.

94 THE RICKSHAW. Mulk Raj Anand, *Coolie*; reprinted by permission of the author, and of Messrs. Lawrence & Wishart Ltd.

95 THE NATIVES OF NEW HOLLAND. Captain James Cook, *The Journal of Captain James Cook*.

96 AN AMERICAN ABROAD. Washington Irving, *The Sketch Book*.

98 MARCO POLO AT THE COURT OF KUBLA KHAN. Marco Polo, *The Travels of Marco Polo*, Book II, translated by William Marsden.

100 EASTER IN JERUSALEM. Lady Sybil Lubbock, *On Ancient Ways*; reprinted by permission of the executors of the author, and of Messrs. Jonathan Cape Ltd.

101 WITHIN THE ORCHID DOOR. Nora Waln, *The House of Exile*; reprinted by permission of the author, and of The Cresset Press Ltd.

103   LIFE IN ADDIS ABABA. L. M. Nesbitt, *Desert and Forest*; reprinted by permission of the executors of the author, and of Messrs. Jonathan Cape Ltd.

104   MAKING AN AFRICAN KING. Paul B. du Chaillu, *Explorations and Adventures in Equatorial Africa*.

105   THE TOTEM. J. Tom Brown, *Among the Bantu Nomads*; reprinted by permission of Messrs. Seeley, Service & Co., Ltd.

106   GIPSIES. John Clare.

      AN EASTERN MAGICIAN. Wilfrid Scawen Blunt, *My Diaries*, Part I; reprinted by permission of the trustees of the author's estate, and of Messrs. Secker & Warburg Ltd.

108   TO EXILES. Neil Munro; reprinted by permission of the trustees of the late Dr. Neil Munro, and of Messrs. William Blackwood & Sons Ltd.

109   IN PASSING. James Howell, *Instructions for forreine travell*, 1642.

113   PLACE NAMES. Sir Osbert Sitwell, *Winters of Content*; reprinted by permission of Messrs. Gerald Duckworth & Co., Ltd.

115   NORWAY'S FJORDS. H. Muir Evans, *Sting Fish and Sea-Farer*; reprinted by permission of Messrs. Faber & Faber Ltd.

116   NORTH LABRADOR. Hart Crane, *The Complete Poems of Hart Crane*; reprinted by permission of the Liveright Publishing Corporation, New York.

      HEBRIDES HOSPITALITY. Samuel Johnson, *A Journey to the Western Islands*.

117   IN ROMNEY MARSH. John Davidson, *The Collected Poems of John Davidson*; reprinted by permission of Messrs. John Lane The Bodley Head Ltd.

118   THE GARDENS OF HOHENHEIM. Friedrich Schiller, *Miscellaneous Writings* (1795).

119   OF GREATHAM. John Drinkwater; reprinted by permission of the poet's representatives, and of Messrs. Sidgwick & Jackson Ltd.

120   CHAMPLAIN'S ACCOUNT OF THE GOUGOU. Samuel de Champlain, from *Purchas his Pilgrims*, edited by Samuel Purchas, the elder.

      THE OTHER ENGLAND. H. E. Bates; reprinted by permission of the author, and of the Editor of *The Spectator*.

121   THE SLAVE PENS OF CAPE LOPEZ. Paul B. du Chaillu, *Explorations and Adventures in Equatorial Africa*.

123   DESERT DAY. Charles M. Doughty, *Travels in Arabia Deserta*.

124   ARABIA. Walter de la Mare; reprinted by permission of the poet, and of Messrs. Faber & Faber Ltd.

      A HOUSE IN THE TYROL. Nina Murdoch, *Tyrolean June*; reprinted by permission of Messrs. George G. Harrap & Co., Ltd.

126   THE APENNINES. Percy Bysshe Shelley.

      THE SPELL OF THE SHETLANDS. Negley Farson, *Way of a Transgressor*; reprinted by permission of the author, and of Messrs. Victor Gollancz Ltd.

127   GIBRALTAR. Richard Chevenix Trench.

128   A TOWN IN SPAIN. Anthony Thorne, *Delay in the Sun*; reprinted by permission of the author, and of Messrs. William Heinemann Ltd.

130   RUE DE LA GAIETÉ. E. Œ. Somerville and Martin Ross, *Stray-Aways*; reprinted by permission of Dr. Somerville, and of Messrs. Longmans, Green, & Co., Ltd.
      THE ENGLISHMAN IN ITALY. Robert Browning, from "The Englishman in Italy".

132   NICOLO ZENO IN ENGRONELAND, 1380. Richard Hakluyt, *The Principal Navigations, etc., of the English Nation.*
      MAJORCA. George Sand (Madame Dudevant), *A Winter in Majorca.*

133   THE EAST. Joseph Conrad, *Youth*; reprinted by permission of the trustees of the Joseph Conrad estate, of Messrs. William Blackwood & Sons Ltd., and of Messrs. J. M. Dent & Sons Ltd.

134   TARANTELLA. Hilaire Belloc; reprinted by permission of Messrs. Gerald Duckworth & Co., Ltd.

135   ON HORSEBACK IN ANDALUSIA. George Borrow, *The Bible in Spain.*

136   GRANTCHESTER. Rupert Brooke, from "The Old Vicarage, Grantchester"; reprinted by permission of the poet's representatives, and of Messrs. Sidgwick & Jackson Ltd.
      TAHITI. Herman Melville, *Omoo.*

137   THE ISLES OF GREECE. Lord Byron, from "The Isles of Greece".

138   UNDER THE EQUATOR. Henry Walter Bates, *A Naturalist on the Amazons.*

139   IN PADUA. William Shakespeare, *The Taming of the Shrew*, Act I, Scene I.

140   THE BAY OF RIO. Herman Melville, *White Jacket.*

142   ON OLD ROME. Philip Ayres.

143   THE RIVER CLITUMNUS. Pliny, from *The Source of the Clitumnus*, Book VIII in the translation by William Melmoth of Pliny's letters.

144   TO AILSA ROCK. John Keats.

147   DEFINITION. John Steinbeck and Edward F. Ricketts, *Sea of Cortez*; reprinted by permission of the authors, and of the Viking Press, New York.
      THE RESCUE. F. D. Ommanney, *South Latitude*; reprinted by permission of Messrs. Longmans, Green, & Co., Ltd.

148   CALONAK ISLAND. Sir John Mandeville, *The Travels of Sir John Mandeville.*

150   OCTHER'S VOYAGE IN THE YEAR 890. Richard Hakluyt, *The Principal Navigations, etc., of the English Nation.*

151   POMPEY'S FLIGHT. Plutarch, from Bernadotte Perrin's translation of Plutarch's *Lives*, published by the Loeb Classical Library, and reprinted by permission of the Publishers.

152   ON SAFARI. W. Lavallin Puxley, *Travels and Adventures in Many Lands*; reprinted by permission of the author, and of Messrs. Williams & Norgate Ltd.